Crowley, Milner & Co.

CROWLEY'S

DETROIT'S Friendly STORE

BRUCE ALLEN KOPYTEK

THE
History
PRESS

Published by The History Press
Charleston, SC
www.historypress.net

Cover images courtesy of the author.

First published 2015

Manufactured in the United States

ISBN 978.1.46711.974.0

Library of Congress Control Number: 2015953416

Notice: The information in this book is true and complete to the best of our knowledge. It is offered without guarantee on the part of the author or The History Press. The author and The History Press disclaim all liability in connection with the use of this book.

Dedicated to my sister, Mary Eve Klamo, and my brother, Patrick Joseph Kopytek—who grew up with me in our Detroit.

CONTENTS

ACKNOWLEDGEMENTS

$\mathcal{G}$iven the lack of specific archives, and the fact that Crowley's disappeared over fifteen years ago, it was clear to me that a book dedicated to the store would require the cooperation of many people from many walks of life. An author with a particular historical interest begins his work without much more than a few memories and perhaps a set of preconceived ideas that must be either confirmed or disproven. When traditional research sources prove inconclusive or nonexistent, a plea goes out, and an author hopes for help. In the case of *Crowley's: Detroit's Friendly Store*, I was assisted by the knowledge, collections and sheer kindness of the following people.

The first proof that I would not work alone came from Carl Katafiasz of the Livonia Public Library, who saved me a trip across town in Detroit's traffic by sending local newspaper articles about Crowley's 1964 opening. Actually, my "best librarian" award with regard to this book is a tie; it also goes to Josh Rouan of the Birmingham Baldwin Library, who likewise supplied me with information it would have otherwise taken days to retrieve. Author Michael Hauser proved to be a great support throughout the development of this book, not just by loaning a whole box full of Crowley memorabilia but also by verifying facts and offering support and numerous suggestions along the way. Likewise, department store historian Kevin Kiepert supplied me with a great deal of background information about Crowley's and Demery's that proved indispensable. Local historian and former Oak Park mayor Jerry Naftaly lent valuable assistance as well. Historian and author Dan

ACKNOWLEDGEMENTS

Austin, who created the magnificent Historic Detroit website, was able to get me access to photographs otherwise unavailable for use and posted a plea for information about Crowley's on his blog. Without any of these people, let me be clear: this book could not exist.

Others who helped deserve the reader's gratitude, as well as mine. Marcy Goldstein of JGA Architects enthusiastically procured images from her employer's archives for my use; Dan Redstone of Redstone Associates opened up the world of his famous firm's photos for my use; and Sue Brooks of the Smith Group (successor architecture firm to Detroit's Smith, Hinchman & Grylls) helped me find information about the building the firm designed for Pardridge & Blackwell and, ultimately, Crowley's. I am also grateful to the Detroit Historical Society and the Manning Brothers Historical Photo Collection for their assistance.

With regard to pictures, I am indebted to Mike Grobbel, who rescued an anonymous box of slides, posted his scans of photos of Crowley's online and was more than willing to let me use the treasure he saved. Thanks go to author Michael Lisicky for the use of his photos as well.

Jack Butler of Chicago and his Detroit-area brother, Keith, enthusiastically answered my call for some information about the store their father owned from 1955 to 1972: Demery's. The book would be lacking good pictures of this part of Crowley's history without their help.

A snowy Sunday afternoon spent over coffee with Steve Kennedy gave me more than insight into Crowley's for the book; it also gave me a peek into the life of this extraordinary man who lived behind the scenes at Detroit's Friendly Store. I am full of gratitude for the generous amount of time he has shared with me. Norine Blake, likewise, enthusiastically shared her Crowley's stories with me and allowed me into her home to talk about the store. At the last minute, Leigh Morrison, the only Crowley family member able to assist with this book, came to my rescue to fill in some facts and offer insight.

Lastly, I must mention my deeply felt appreciation for my lovely wife, Carole, for putting up with my obsession with the story of Crowley, Milner & Co.; for her proofreading skills; her continuous encouragement; and, most of all, her love, affection and understanding.

1
MY DETROIT

I can never go back to my Detroit, that's for sure. It doesn't exist anymore, and as time goes by, even the tiniest vestiges of it seem to have vanished at an alarming rate. Only my own memories of my Detroit exist, just like someone's memories of old Berlin before it was bombed into oblivion or ancient Rome before it was ransacked by barbarians.

My Detroit thrives in my mind as I reminisce about the past, but even these memories soften and lose focus after so many years. My Detroit might have been like the Detroit that others recall, but they, too, can never return to it physically because it simply isn't there any longer. For some, the Detroit they call "theirs" (like the one I call "mine") is too difficult to visit even in the vast world of memory. It can be painful to recall a place that is gone forever. Some even deny that it ever existed at all, claiming that it was nothing more tangible than a mirage on a hot, desert-like day. Still others reminisce more happily, stoically admonishing the old saying "Nothing good lasts forever."

How did my Detroit look? My Detroit wasn't a city cut into isolated pieces by the broad, vacant swaths of expressways (though they were being conceived and built at the time). It wasn't a city of glassy, outrageous or jagged-shaped buildings. It wasn't even so tall that it inhabited the record books, at least during my lifetime. It was a city of smooth, honed corners and worn bricks. It was old (in reality, Old World) but with a charm that is perhaps its most tragically forgotten aspect; indeed, it is this elusive charm that refuses to surface in any clarity, no matter how hard memory tries to conjure it. It is the charm of little corners, interesting perspectives and burnished images rendered in deep, rich colors placed between the blue of the sky and the varied, Ireland-like greens that covered the earth in my Detroit.

Because I was a young one when I inhabited my Detroit, it seemed like the center of the world. Even after traveling to places much bigger and more important, it was always possible to compare them favorably with the town described by pop radio jingles as "the Motor City." It had a river (boy, did it ever!); it had skyscrapers—the Penobscot Building being the tallest, which I learned to recognize after my mother pointed out the illuminated red ball surmounting a conical tower at its peak. It had a palatial city hall and courthouse, and almost more importantly, it had what we now call "infill." This infill didn't look too important, yet it provided a place for life to exist between all of these monuments. Look at pictures of my Detroit (if you can find them) and you will not see isolated buildings surrounded by parking lots, puddled by the most recent rainfall and strewn with shards of broken glass. Instead, little, old and even shabby buildings formed edges, or "walls," that defined streets and connected various landmarks. I almost forgot to add that in between those important and not-so-important landmarks were the numerous leafy green spaces up to which the streets led.

The names of these streets—Woodward, Randolph, Griswold, Gratiot, Jefferson—and the squares like Grand Circus Park (in my Detroit, you could call a half circle a "square") gave importance and meaning to the places my parents took me. When I lived in my Detroit, I was young and didn't have a care in the world, much less a curiosity for those imposing names and what they meant. To a young boy, it was all so big as to almost be incomprehensible.

I lived on a typical street in my Detroit. My Detroit had a lot of boundaries, real and perceived. Our neat little post–World War II brick bungalow sat on an emerald-green lawn of bent grass, meticulously cared for by my father; he trimmed its sidewalk edges by hand, on his hands and knees, so that it looked like the "whitewalls" that were an aspect of a typically-popular haircut of the day, with well-defined trimming around the ears. Anything beyond this lawn was not our property but the city's (yet my dad maintained it all so that it looked like it was ours). The garden in back of our house had its own set of boundaries, and for good reason. Behind the garage and at the back was the alley where my neighbors burnt paper in wire baskets and where, weekly, the garbage truck grinded and squeaked along, stopping, starting and swallowing up garbage. Our fence, utterly the same as any other in my Detroit, separated our garden from the alley and from our neighbors' yards. This silvery boundary (exceptionally so when my father painted it and returned to the house to wash up spattered in silver paint) wasn't a negative thing—our neighbors in my Detroit were cherished and welcome at any time in our home or yard. The fence simply said "this is mine, and that is yours," and gave security to children and safety and comfort to pets, even if they—like Rusty, our neighbor's dog—acted like they'd run like hell and bring terror to any youngsters they encountered if they could get only past the gates.

In my youngest years, I could not venture past these boundaries, but the rule was that after age twelve, I could ride my bike in and across the streets (assuming I practiced the safety rules taught by my parents) that crisscrossed our little neighborhood. The big roads, like Six Mile to the south and Seven Mile to the north, were even bigger boundaries that demanded permission or parental accompaniment to venture beyond.

Church and school in my Detroit were one and the same, local and accessible because they were only four short blocks from home. Our church, the now vacant Our Lady of Good Counsel, had its own boundaries (defined by lawns, flowerbeds with statues and a small parking lot) as well. In my Detroit, you most often walked or rode a bike from place to place. On Sunday mornings, we walked to church past numerous similar houses with gardens and fences, walkways and porches. In all of this, I cannot focus so much on my Detroit's physical aspects that I forget that there was more often than not a smiling face tending the flowers, cutting the lawn or just relaxing on a glider on a porch, eager to say hello or ask about my family. My Detroit was a community of close-knit neighbors enjoying the same experience of life on that little patch of earth.

My Detroit had its own sounds and smells. I could often smell the cooking of my German American neighbor to the south, and on hot summer evenings, the smell of boiling mash from the Strohs' brewery filled the air. Not too far away, the Better Made Potato Chip factory, the one with a lift that could tilt a truck of spuds forty-five degrees into the air for quick unloading, emitted a heavenly aroma that couldn't be avoided and, more often than not, aroused one's taste buds and caused an intense craving for the locally made treat.

Above, the sound of airplanes was almost continual and certainly unavoidable, since the city airport was only blocks away. The racket of one of GM's large airliners in takeoff might have seemed like a nuisance to strangers, but to us, it was normal and hardly worth noting. In the 1960s, the sound of my Detroit was often touched by sadness because I could not play in the painted sandbox, crafted especially for me by my parents, without hearing the regular twenty-one-gun salutes for the country's war dead. The sounds of my Detroit carried all sorts of meanings and emotions day in and day out. I believe some would find it strange that an occasional evening pastime in my Detroit was to walk or ride over to see the site of a small plane crash right in my neighborhood. The scene of a turquoise Piper Cub being hauled out of a tree by a crane resides in my memory, much as a preserved thirty-five-millimeter slide sits in a file-box, waiting to be seen again when it is pulled from its slot.

My Detroit was a place of celebrations, which often bound family and neighbors, if only for a moment. I was fortunate to have parents who were keen on travel, especially a father who documented our journeys with his Bell & Howell camera. On some warm, starlit nights after our return from these trips, Dad would erect a screen out back in the garden (the one bordered not just by the aforementioned fence but also by my mother's lovingly cared for roses and lilies) and run an extension cord through a bedroom window to power the projector. It seemed that the whole neighborhood came over, some bringing folding lawn chairs, to watch films of places they could only hope to visit. Mom put out soft drinks and snacks (and maybe some beer for the men), and our backyard was transformed into a homemade cinema, just for one evening.

Other warm-weather celebrations included trips to one or more of the local amusement parks that flourished for years in my Detroit. Many of my family members took an annual trip to Bob-Lo Island, mostly because of the gorgeous steamer ride down the river to reach it. Dad, being a navy veteran, never lost his interest in ships, so I was cognizant of the fact that he loved watching the innumerable lake freighters and oceangoing ships pass by our front-row deck seats on the SS *Columbia* or *Ste. Claire* in spite of his intention to "take the kids out'da island and put 'em on some rides." Interestingly enough, there was no grand gateway or terminal in my Detroit to signify the pleasure and uniqueness of the steamer trip to Bob-Lo, just a humble pavilion on the old, industrial waterfront (at the "foot of Woodward") huddled between ancient buildings and possessed of scrolled cast-iron brackets supporting its pigeon-inhabited roof. Those cage-like turnstiles allowed pleasure-seekers toting picnic hampers and ice chests a bit of shelter before one of the steamers' deafening whistles signaled that they should be aboard for the cruise down the river to the mouth of Lake Erie that would begin in five minutes.

Edgewater Park, though it had a rough-riding wooden roller coaster that Bob-Lo didn't, was a little too far to visit frequently, lying across my Detroit's east-west dividing line of Woodward Avenue. Distant Walled Lake was simply out of the question, even though Mom remembered going dancing there "with your dad and his brothers before the war."

These places were not really regional destinations but local ones, simple places that were not the products of an imagineer's mind but green spaces that provided entertainment and gritty fun on a regular basis for the nearby residents of cities like my Detroit. Unbelievably (to someone who grew up in my Detroit), not just the physicality of these amusement parks but their very ideas and reasons for being, have completely disappeared and almost don't make sense any more. A park in a neighborhood where families can go to relax and have a few good-natured laughs or dance in a ballroom to a live orchestra currently has no *raison d'être*, but in my Detroit, it surely did.

Other summer pleasures of my Detroit—like an evening ride out to Belle Isle to breathe the fresh air on the waterfront—were simpler, but some were truly big events. The Independence Day fireworks display sponsored by "our" J.L. Hudson department store was certainly one of the latter. We had to leave home with a picnic dinner prepared by my mother in hand as soon as my father returned home from work at "his" factory. Timing was essential to getting a grassy spot along the main waterfront, where we ate, listened to big-band music and waited for the big show to begin. The first syncopated bangs of the huge white bombs that lit up the night and echoed off the tall buildings brought on a sense of simultaneous terror and delight that can be difficult to describe; you just had to be there in my Detroit.

The Gold Cup Unlimited hydroplane races were another unique warm-weather event. My mom would sometimes drive my dad to work at the Bower Roller Bearing Company factory near the waterfront race course so we could watch the time trials during the day and pick him up on the way home. There were few time constraints on Sunday, race day, since our only obligation was to get to early Mass so we could come home and change into more casual clothing for the daylong outing to the riverfront.

Lest anyone think that recreational activities in my Detroit were limited to the summer, I can assure you that they were not. Cold weather was celebrated in a state whose license plates were emblazoned with the slogan "Water Winter Wonderland" in those days. For my parents' part, they built an ice-skating rink (ringed with real boards since my dad was a carpenter before taking on factory work after the war) in our back yard, and a beautiful two-toned toboggan that spent the summer in the rafters of our garage came out of hibernation (if you could call it that). We took the toboggan on numerous runs down Derby Hill a bit to the west of our home on the elegant Outer Drive, which, in addition to being lined with lovely homes, had many parks along its circuitous route through my Detroit.

There were also winter specialty places in my Detroit. Often, after the Thanksgiving dishes were washed and put away and perhaps a second round of turkey was eaten, my dad would offer to take us downtown to see the lights. Aunt Stella, who hosted the affair—which was once called a "Roman orgy of food" by a college friend who joined us one year—was able to come with us in our nine-passenger station wagon and joined in the collective oohs and aahs as we drove through the downtown streets, culminating at the giant J.L. Hudson store on Woodward that displayed a twelve-story tree of strung lights on its deep red brick façade. The nighttime journey was somehow made even more magical by the illuminated windows at the base of these large stores that lined the streets, often under deep marquees with displays above them; Crowley's glimmering white building offered shelter, welcome and a chance for passersby to experience desire (while looking at the displays).

Returning home via the scenic route along Jefferson Avenue past the mansions of Grosse Pointe (where my uncle Edmund said all the "rich dudes" lived), we might stop at Eastland to admire the more low-key holiday displays at that fairly new and very swanky shopping center. My Detroit, or at least the distant part of it, better known as Dearborn, had something unique for us, too, in the form of the Ford Rotunda, a vestige of the 1933–34 Chicago World's Fair: an Art Deco wedding cake of a building, brilliantly illuminated, that housed a carnival inside it at Christmastime, which afforded me yet another visit to Santa, and rides and whimsical displays that seemed simply out of this world to a youngster of the day. Years later, after the Rotunda burned and was never replaced, it saddened me to think it was gone, for it's otherworldly appearance when lit at night might have been the first time I ever saw a building that took my breath away by reason of its sheer audacity and one-of-a-kind quality.

To fulfill the everyday needs of families like mine, my Detroit had shopping facilities. Just walking a block to the end of our street put us within reach of a delicatessen, an ice cream parlor, a party store, a fruit market and a small carry-out place named Chicken Delight where I could get a bag of French fries for five cents. Not a single one of these places in my Detroit were part of large national chains. We knew the owners (like Ziggy from the delicatessen or Mr. Skladd, who owned the party store), and they knew us by name; they were fixtures of my Detroit. More varied needs were met in the neighborhood but required a bike ride, a long walk, a bus ride or a trip in the car. Waltham's drugstore and Alinosi's ice cream parlor weren't that far away. Being Polish American, my mother bought our required ethnic specialties (usually in conjunction with a trip to visit my grandmother) in nearby Hamtramck. My Detroit was very diverse, so I am sure others did likewise. The local fruit market was owned by Italians, but my neighbors, friends and schoolmates recognized themselves as being of Irish, Scottish, German, Hungarian, Belgian, Dutch, French or Lebanese descent, and many simply saw themselves as American.

Farther afield, my Detroit was composed of local shopping districts that stretched out along major streets, like the one we patronized on Gratiot Avenue at Seven Mile Road, where a local Federal department store shared the street with an elegantly detailed brick-and-stone Montgomery Ward store. In between there were other shops, and not far away, closer to home at Six Mile, was the palatial Ramona theater, whose white-haired ticket lady could always be seen in her curved-glass enclosure below the flashy marquee that wrapped around the corner.

Of course, there were many other options for shopping and entertainment, including Eastland, only a one-transfer bus ride away, but for something special, the center of my Detroit was the place to be. When my mother offered to sew my sister's wedding gown, we sought out a warehouse-like store of six or seven floors, risking the ride up a clanking, dusty old elevator that stopped at floor after floor chock-full of bolts of sewing material of any description. For once, the fabric department in the basement of Neisner's or some obscure Hamtramck shop wasn't good enough for mom; not until she measured and inspected the requisite crêpe, lace, silk, veiling and trim (approved, of course, by the future bride) could we dare to leave that unassuming and ancient warehouse and the treasures it held within.

Another suspect elevator ride occurred when my aunt accompanied my siblings and me downtown to see *2001: A Space Odyssey* at the Summit Cinerama theater. The nearby parking garage was a dark, almost spooky place to have to contend with before entering the cinema proper. If the neighborhood theater wasn't showing a particular film, or if there was to be a shopping/lunch/film excursion, my Detroit's downtown was ideal, for it offered entertainment and eating options concentrated in an area that, at the time, required dressing up for the event. My Detroit's Michigan Theater struck me as the most incredible of these cavernous pleasure palaces with its grand staircases, magnificent promenades, chandeliers and ceilings worthy of some European royal palace. What's more, its curvaceous, pipe organ–augmented interiors, which intrigued and inspired a boy destined to become an architect, went completely dark when the feature film (or the preceding cartoons) began, and the hundreds of patrons sat together watching the big screen that made the black-and-white films seem larger than life.

Although a trip into the center of my Detroit might be for a specialist doctor visit or some other mundane task, it was most often undertaken for the sheer pleasure of shopping. Indeed, the long bus ride in a GM coach, replete with the squeaking and rattling of the bus (which seemed to float over the roadway with its bumps, exposed cobbles and streetcar tracks) and the sound of the "next stop, please" gong, helped build excitement as the vehicle descended Gratiot Avenue toward the mass of buildings that rose in a pyramidal shape, forming the center of my Detroit. Indeed, as the passing neighborhoods gave way to taller buildings and downtown approached, a large sign projecting from the façade of the eponymous department store and consisting of red letters in white, illuminated squares spelling out C-R-O-W-L-E-Y-S vertically, came into view, and the ultimate goal was near.

My Detroit had a lot to offer the shopper, from large stores like Crowley's and Hudson's (and Kern's before that) to smaller shops, many of which paraded up Woodward Avenue from the hard-to-define square known as Campus Martius, extending even to Grand Boulevard to the north. In between, dime stores (concentrated on the west side of Woodward), restaurants, hotels, theaters, drugstores and any other imaginable type of retail operation jostled for attention. It was the big stores, though, that set the tone for my Detroit's downtown.

The city was fortunate to have a world-famous department store to dominate its retail business, for that store was truly a style setter. All someone had to say was "I'm going to Hudson's" or "I got it at Hudson's," and class, cachet and exclusivity were well and truly implied. It was a physical presence as well; the hulking, yet exquisitely detailed mass of brick with travertine trim at the ground level and countless display windows punctuated by shiny aluminum-and-glass entries with door handles emblazoned with the letters "JLH" in script, left no doubt that this was someplace special. No one could pass through my Detroit and, looking at its onetime unique skyline, fail to notice the tall red brick tower (looking like a square turret of an oversized medieval castle) looming high above the mass of many less famous buildings, proclaiming "HUDSON'S" on each of its four sides in enormous white letters that were outlined in red neon at night.

Since I came from a family not too far removed from its immigrant background, Hudson's was just a bit too much for our regular needs. My mother felt much more at home in its subterranean two-level budget store and only ventured upstairs for special occasions. These included the time preceding my sister's wedding (the event of the century to our little family, one that was only equaled by her graduation from the University of Detroit a few years earlier, the first with our name to do so) or at Christmastime. More often than not, it was to see the brilliant wonderland the store created in its auditorium to delight children and put adults in the mood for shopping, but I can recall the Christmas that I told Santa (and my parents) that the item I'd like more than anything was a toy roller coaster. My parents knew that Hudson's was the only store with the variety and breadth of stock that might satiate their little son's eccentric dreams. So, a walk through the aisles and aisles of counters and tables with toys of every description was made, in a somewhat clandestine manner, pointing out not one but three examples of such a toy in order to glean my preferences for the item that would ultimately wind up under the tree to the delight of one little resident of my Detroit.

Kern's was, sadly, before my time (though mother spoke well of it, having patronized the store in her Detroit), but Crowley's doorstep was well-worn by our family. We preferred it for the very reasons it was different from its august and more famous neighbor: it was more homelike, friendly and clearly without the pretentions that Hudson's nurtured as a matter of fact. Its basement was just that, a place for bargains, while its general price points were lower (and to my mother's liking), especially when the store had a sale. Its interior appointments were not unglamorous but warm and burnished, somewhat showing their age but welcoming nonetheless.

No resident of my Detroit forgot the difference between Hudson's and Crowley's when going from floor-to-floor inside of the cavernous, airy and light-colored store. The well-remembered wooden escalators, which wobbled and clanked along, were a true contrast to Hudson's sleek, speedy, shiny stainless-steel conveyances. Perhaps the stores' other mode of vertical transportation, its elevators, were similar—but Hudson's had many, many more of them. In spite of it all, or perhaps because of it all, my Detroit had a special place in its heart for Crowley's. My Detroit without Hudson's towering above its core was unthinkable, but losing Crowley's would have conjured up sincere feelings of sadness by anyone who frequented the place.

So, if these descriptions are accurate, just when did my Detroit disappear? It wasn't the result of an instant cataclysm but more the result of time itself, something like the proverbial frog slowly being boiled alive without realizing it. Even I, as such an observant resident (and now chronicler) of my Detroit, can't pinpoint the moment that it ceased to exist. Rather, there were hints, signs and events that I might have noticed at the time, but I, too, was in the slowly boiling water along with my Detroit itself.

There were, to be sure, events that were harbingers of the death of my Detroit. Certainly, one of them was the big riot of 1967. Oh, sure, my mom and dad talked about the 1943 riot and how it began on their wedding day, but the kindly Hamtramck firemen across the street from their reception saved it from being shut down by the police through their offer to "keep an eye on" the celebration and make sure nothing untoward happened. The city went on to prosper after the earlier riots, so why should the 1967 version be any different? It was different. We really never locked our doors before that time, and I never saw panic in my parents' faces as when the event grew from a small news report into something that came too close for comfort. From our house, you could hear the shots and smell the smoke, and my sister almost got caught in the middle of it on the day it started. It was hot and, for the first time, I was told to close and lock the windows while I slept. To an eight-year-old-boy—the son of a man who could fix anything—panic took over and the nights were spent worrying how strong that glass in those locked windows really was, and how it couldn't possibly keep anything out, especially the thing that had the ability to destroy whole city blocks…

Maybe they didn't make it into the national news, but seemingly insignificant events heralded the gradual disappearance of my Detroit. Downtown shopping trips weren't curtailed so much by the presence of new malls in the suburbs (the downtown stores were huge and had better selections, after all) but by the fact that one of my sister's friends had an unpleasant encounter while waiting for a bus outside of Hudson's. From the time of that ugly event, the approach to shopping was to go downtown only if it warranted it and only if a sufficient party could be assembled to ensure safety in numbers. News of a stabbing death right in Hudson's didn't do anything to encourage us, either.

I know that as a child, I perceived a definite sense of loss when—after numerous warm summer evenings spent on Belle Isle on a blanket with my parents, sister and brother, aunts and uncles listening to the great Detroit Concert Band under director Leonard B. Smith—we heard that the concerts were stopped after being disrupted by near riots fomented by youth who didn't appreciate them. We'd have to look elsewhere and, in fact, inward for that kind of enjoyment as my Detroit slipped away. I will always recall the delight in my mom's expression as she admonished me to "listen closely—they're going to play 'Flight of the Bumblebee' next!" In my Detroit, enjoyment didn't seem to be the result of intoxication or even raw exhilaration, but of betterment, knowledge and culture.

My Detroit began to look deteriorated after the riots, too. It seemed that there wasn't a great deal anymore that was new and worthwhile; you had to go out to the suburbs for that, and much of it seemed either ramshackle or very isolated, overtly commercial and in a state of deterioration. Downtown, the seedy Kern block had become dirty and old, so, along with a number of notable buildings, it was simply erased from the map. The resultant open space was a lawn with sidewalks that reminded the residents of my Detroit of the Chrysler "Pentastar" logo when seen in aerial photographs.

But this cavity (cavities, really) at the heart of my Detroit was more than just an unusual shape. Of course, Crowley's had the light of day shone on it like never before, but the open space was too much and too vast, and in addition to spoiling the spatial continuity of my Detroit, it attracted loiterers and pointed to the sad fact that the city was crumbling from within.

I couldn't help taking less ownership of my Detroit on the day my aunt Stella called after 11:00 p.m. when she came home from her afternoon shift as a supervisor at the Champion Spark Plug factory to find her house ransacked and burglarized. Of course, an immediate family trip to her side for comfort and support produced a telling sentiment: how could something like this happen in my Detroit? It had never happened to us before. I should have known, but my Detroit was slipping away. The very same thing happened to her a total of three times in one year, before she moved away out of fear. In fact, the same thing happened to our own home twice in the coming years. It's difficult to call a place with such disrespect for people and their families home. Prior to that time, our doors were unlocked more often than not; now the reverse was true.

The downward spiral got steeper on the day that Jan, one of my university teaching assistants, was shot to death sitting in a car on the first Saturday evening after school began in 1977. Being from New York, he enjoyed the amenities and unique spaces that characterize the best urban environments, so one Saturday evening, he drove to sit and watch the beautiful Scott fountain on Belle Isle as its cascading water features (and ensuing cool breezes) were illuminated like so many colors and flavors of icing dripping down an elaborate, albeit marble, torte. He didn't know, however, that our family had long ago stopped going there; it didn't seem safe anymore. For Jan's lack of knowledge, he was rewarded with a bullet to the head that killed him on the spot. Witnesses there were aplenty, but not one witness chose to reveal who the shooter was. The crime was never solved. My Detroit was now speeding away as fast as a bullet.

Soon, it seemed that practically every aspect of what made my Detroit a one-of-a-kind place disappeared. In terms of a single human life, it happened gradually; in terms of history, it was fast. It was not so fast as the falling of a catastrophic bomb but was relentless and devastating in its effect just the same. The history of the city of Detroit was one of meteoric rise, great growth and prosperity in the first half of the twentieth century. Post mid-1960s, my Detroit came crashing toward calamity at a meteoric rate, wiping out all before it.

It seemed only the God-given physical aspects remained, along with a few of the man-made ones, but the heart, the life and the best of it were gone. They all followed one another one by one. The amusement parks disappeared. Unbelievably, that summer trademark, a boat-trip to Bob-Lo Island, slipped into the past, too. Downtown's once-grand hotels became flophouses, withered or closed until they disappeared from the landscape or sat like skeletons on the ever-broadening horizon. Outside downtown, whole neighborhoods disappeared or evolved over time into "urban prairies" after abused homes burned, collapsed or were bulldozed because they, once the home of a family like mine in my Detroit, became health and safety hazards.

Familiar places were no more. Of course, there was always something new in the suburbs, but that was just the problem: it was something new, a flash-in-the-pan, something whose time would come one day as well. The old, familiar and, it has to be said, human character was gone. As my Detroit sank into the ocean of neglect like some stricken transatlantic liner, it was clear that a civic meltdown was happening right in our midst.

Nowhere was this degeneration more apparent than the downtown area where once we shopped, relaxed by the waterfront or were entertained by movies. The movie houses closed after years of offering questionable fare to varying degrees of questionable clientele. The pervasive smell of urine in them, the grime, filth and vandalism assaulted the senses and made once-pleasant visits matters of resignation. "Let's not go there anymore!" we cried. Detroit's three railroad terminals, disused and neglected, crumbled and even disappeared, meeting the wrecking ball faster than a property owner could calculate the revenue to be generated by a parking lot.

My Detroit's "warts and all" were suddenly front and center for the world to see. Detroit's defining physical element, the river, had long been a commercial and industrial area before planning commissions sought City Beautiful redevelopments to give a different character to the waterfront. These plans, notably the 1924 venture by Finnish American architect Eliel Saarinen—even more so the one he proposed, with his son Eero, after World War II—sought to de-commercialize, de-industrialize and de-historicize the historic cradle of the city. However, just like the 1805 plan of Detroit by Augustus Woodward, that gave the city a geometric regularity practically unique in city planning, no single beautification scheme was fully embraced.

The postwar Saarinen and Saarinen example was bitten, chewed up and spat out in the form of a few isolated buildings—notably a windowless auditorium, a near-windowless but enormous convention center and a memorial office building for the Veterans' Administration—plunked on the riverfront not differently from the brick warehouses they sought to replace. The space in between was relegated to secondary status, no more than parking lots and freeway interchanges, until the bleak and artistically vapid Hart plaza opened in the early 1980s.

Nothing spelt the end of my Detroit like the disappearance of its department stores and the decay of the Woodward Avenue shopping area, though the neglect, death and eventual removal of the great elm trees that lined my street (and made it look like a lofty but natural and foliage-encrusted cathedral) ran a close second place. The first victim downtown, of course, was Crowley's in 1977. The store that once prided itself on being "friendly" turned its back on the city and its own past, and it was just a matter of time before the world-famous Hudson's, that iconic Detroit store that everyone believed "would always be there," succumbed six years later. My Detroit no longer held much attraction, and its transferal from reality into memory became inexorable.

Years and years later, it's nostalgic to remember the names and places of my Detroit. So many things crowd the memory of it: the lost Tiger Stadium; long-gone Olympia, where Gordie Howe and the Red Wings had their greatest successes; simple places like the Vernor's Ginger Ale factory; and the Art Deco Chrysler showroom on Jefferson Avenue at Connor, where we waited each fall for the curtains to open, revealing yearly the spectacular new Chrysler models that would make us proud to say we lived, worked and played in my Detroit.

Remembering Crowley, Milner & Co., one of Detroit's saddest losses (both the store itself as well as the classic, beautiful and underappreciated building that housed it), isn't always an easy process. To recall and appreciate Detroit's Friendly Store requires an understanding of its context and the people who made it the success story it was for almost seventy years in downtown Detroit. Yet for all the things we can no longer do in the city I called my Detroit, we can at least remember, reminisce and try with the power of recollection to bring the great, almost human, store back to life in our minds if not in reality.

2

"FORGET ALL YOUR TROUBLES, FORGET ALL YOUR CARES..."

*G*reat cities are composed of many things. Of course, there is the human element with so many people bustling about doing the daily business of a metropolis like Detroit. Yet the buildings and spaces that house the activities of a city, with the aid of inherent natural characteristics, define the physical space that is the setting for all of this activity. This inherent space gives cities form and defines their *genus loci*. Most historical American cities are given this form by fairly functional structures that, along with green space and circulation patterns, become representative of the place under consideration. Typically, these structures are augmented by great railroad terminals, representative metropolitan hotels, massive department stores and civic buildings like monumental courthouses and museums. Detroit had them all.

The circulation plan of Detroit is, at its core, based on the 1805 plan forwarded by Augustus Woodward and developed on a hexagonal grid. When the city leaders could not see to the plan's pure implementation, fragments of it remained in place when a standard grid pattern was superimposed on it to foster civic growth. The broad avenues that lead out from the center of Detroit—Gratiot, Woodward, Grand River, Michigan Avenues and Fort Street—are lasting vestiges of the earlier plan that have continued to direct the outward growth of the region.

In spite of Detroit's many broad avenues and leafy boulevards, Woodward Avenue became the unquestionable ceremonial artery of Detroit, and the

Woodward Avenue in its heyday. Looking north toward Grand Circus Park, the "west wall" of the street formed a familiar environment for Detroit shoppers. *Courtesy of Dan Redstone, Redstone Associates.*

city grew from its beginning at the Detroit River toward the north. In time, Woodward Avenue unquestionably dominated the city's retail trade, too, though it was not inconceivable that major retail facilities might be located off it. For instance, Hudson's—though it began in small quarters in Detroit's Opera House on Campus Martius, just off Woodward—located its first big retail expansion on Farmer Street, away from the avenue. Tony Washington Boulevard, though it was primarily known as a home to railroad and airline offices, had a reputation for high-end retail, while some Woodward Avenue shops closer to Grand Circus Park, the hub of the spoke-like street arrangement, had entrances on both Woodward and Washington Boulevard.

Detroit's rail terminals, so important to the city in the twentieth century, were, for the most part, outside the downtown core. True, the Canadian-owned Grand Trunk Western Railway had a small, nondescript station near the riverfront downtown, but the city's other two, Union Depot and the Michigan Central Station, were located so a cab or bus ride was necessary to reach them. Union Depot, the older of the two, was located on West

Fort Street and was potentially walkable to the central business district. The rail terminal, as its name indicated, served the Wabash, Chesapeake & Ohio and Pennsylvania Railroads from its sturdy, red brick and sandstone, Richardsonian Romanesque exterior.

The larger and more elaborate Michigan Central Station was built by the New York Central Railroad and its subsidiaries as a major east–west terminal serving its northernmost line between New York City and Chicago, one that cut through Canada and required a tunnel under the Detroit River. The terminal—the work of the associated architects Warren and Wetmore of New York and Reed and Stem of St. Paul, Minnesota—consisted of an eighteen-story office tower that rose above an incredible three-story train concourse modeled after the ancient Baths of Caracalla in Rome. In addition to famous east–west New York Central trains like the Wolverine and the Detroiter to New York City or the Twilight Limited and the Mercury to Chicago, the station serviced Baltimore and Ohio trains to Washington, D.C., as well as the Canadian Pacific Railway.

Most of the Motor City's hotels of note inhabited and enriched the central core of Detroit. Pride of place among these was certainly held by the 1915 Statler Hotel, which occupied a grand location at the corner of Washington Boulevard and Grand Circus Park. The third of Ellsworth M. Statler's famous chain of hotels, the Detroit Statler was later gobbled up by the Hilton organization. The wedge-shaped brick-and-limestone Neo Renaissance pile was the epitome of a grand American metropolitan hotel in many ways, including its varied dining and entertainment options, like its famous Terrace Room and, later, Café Rouge.

At the other end of Washington Boulevard, at Michigan Avenue, rose the massive Sheraton-Cadillac Hotel, an imposing thirty-three-story yellow brick-and-stone skyscraper capped with copper ziggurat pavilions at its corners. The interior spaces of the hotel were among the most spectacular in the city, including an Italian garden and a magnificent ballroom dripping with plaster ornamentation. The Book-Cadillac Hotel was built by Detroit's Book brothers. After building the Book Building across the boulevard, they replaced an eponymous 1885 hostelry, and the lively hotel became a favorite of presidents and sports figures, in no small part due to the hospitality of its Motor Bar and Book Casino restaurants.

Other hotels, such as the Fort Shelby (later a part of the Albert Pick hotel chain), the Tuller and the Detroit-Leland, were spread through the central business district and took up the slack from the more famous places. Another Detroit hotel, the Norton, had a twin (in ownership if not in physicality)

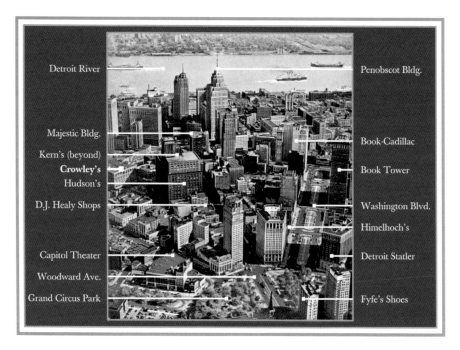

Detroit River	Penobscot Bldg.
Majestic Bldg.	Book-Cadillac
Kern's (beyond)	
Crowley's	Book Tower
Hudson's	
D.J. Healy Shops	Washington Blvd.
	Himelhoch's
Capitol Theater	Detroit Statler
Woodward Ave.	
Grand Circus Park	Fyfe's Shoes

Detroit's unique geometry was easily visible in aerial photographs, but urban renewal, the proliferation of parking lots (where buildings once stood) and newer buildings that don't reinforce the concept have made it a vastly different place than illustrated here. *From a postcard, collection of the author.*

across the river in Windsor and served customers something unique in the city at the time—a river view—from its 1918 construction until its 1959 demolition to make way for the new Michigan Consolidated Gas Building.

Like the hotels, the theaters of Detroit spread throughout and beyond the downtown area. These grand movie palaces, where Detroiters came to be entertained, star-struck or just to escape the monotony of their daily lives, were built as the era of "talking" motion pictures and Hollywood notoriety gained popularity. Generally speaking, as the movie palaces were built, they followed a pattern that moved the entertainment area of the city away from the waterfront and the Campus Martius, another of the hubs of Detroit's spoke-like street system, and closer to the semicircular open space of Grand Circus Park.

The Capitol Theater on Broadway is generally regarded as the first of the theaters that sought, in appointment and sheer size, to become an escape in itself. The four thousand–plus seat colossus was soon followed by the Palms (named after Belgian American Detroit real estate developer

Francis Palms, grandfather of the Book brothers), and both opened in 1925. The Palms and its integral office building were built on Woodward Avenue north of Grand Circus Park and, along with the nearby five-thousand-seat Fox Theater, helped define a shopping, entertainment and retail area that included the well-regarded Fyfe shoe store and a number of elegant residential and transient hotels nearby.

A further concentration of movie palaces was developed on Bagley Avenue, west of Washington Boulevard, in 1928 with the opening of the two thousand–seat United Artists Theater, which had an eighteen-story office tower integrated into the structure. The United Artists Theater building, along with the eight hundred–room Detroit-Leland Hotel were a part of a scheme to improve Bagley Avenue in the 1920s. Detroit's grandest and most over-the-top movie palace was a part of this plan as well.

The four thousand–seat Michigan Theater of 1926 had an extravagance and richness that would hardly be believed today were pictures of it unavailable. Rivalling the Palace of Versailles for opulence of décor, the theater was composed of marble, gilded plaster and sculptural groups that would be commonplace in some European royal residences but were surprising to the common moviegoer in the Motor City. Its promenade, linking its amply arched Bagley Avenue entrance with another access point on Middle Street, was theatrical itself in its conception and modeled after the Hall of Mirrors at Versailles.

Legitimate theater in Detroit, prior to the establishment of today's Fisher Theatre in the New Center area's Fisher Building, was provided by the Shubert-Lafayette Theater on Lafayette Avenue West at Shelby Street. The theater, first opened in 1914 as a cinema named Orpheum, was enhanced by richly colored murals executed by the noted twentieth-century illustrator and artist Maxfield Parrish. At one time, the Shubert organization also operated a Shubert-Detroit Theater in the old Detroit Opera House on Campus Martius.

Detroit's Old City Hall stood guard to the south on Woodward Avenue at the Campus Martius, with the correspondingly monumental County Building on the opposite end of Lafayette Square, another of Detroit's spoke arteries widened to incorporate green space. The old public library, on Farmer Street across from Hudson's 1896 "Big Store" and kitty-corner from Crowley's, was replaced as a branch library in 1932 after the main library itself moved north along Woodward in 1921. Likewise, the Detroit Institute of Arts moved from its old Jefferson Avenue location to a vast and palatial home, designed by noted French architect Paul Cret, across from the new library on Woodward Avenue in 1927.

*Beginning Saturday, September 1 ~ In a new Building
with almost doubled Facilities for Service to our Customers*

47TH ANNIVERSARY
THE J. L. HUDSON COMPANY

By the time Hudson's opened its 1928 building and the familiar Hudson Tower, the store had just about filled a large downtown block and became a formidable competitor to Crowley's. *Collection of the author.*

In a way that is difficult to understand today, downtown Detroit offered something different to the residents of the city. It wasn't just a facility, a building or even a cluster of buildings. It was a spatial and civic ensemble that garnered its own sense of place and had a place in the hearts of its users. As such, every little aspect of it was subservient to the whole and played a part in creating a desirable atmosphere. Unlike today's shopping malls, downtown offered everything in one place, allowing shopping, dining, tourism and entertainment to create a synergism that is all but forgotten. Detroit's Woodward Avenue and the blocks adjacent to it provided all that anyone in Detroit could want, need or hope to find. It did so with an incredible variety of options for concurrent activities that was unique and made it the shopping and entertainment powerhouse of the region.

Above all, the whole downtown district was the premier shopping area of Detroit, and Crowley's was near to, if not directly at, its epicenter. Of the big stores, Hudson's was certainly the major attraction downtown and, arguably, Detroit's favorite department store. The enormous red brick emporium sat directly on Woodward Avenue, and at almost two and a half million square feet of space, it was one of the three largest department store buildings in the world (the other two were R.H. Macy & Co. of New York and Marshall Field & Company of Chicago). The famous and highly visible Hudson Tower added to the store in 1928 made it, at twenty-five stories, the tallest department store in the world as well.

The story of how Joseph Lowthian Hudson came to the United States from Newcastle, England, via Hamilton, Ontario, is well documented in many excellent histories of the company. Most agree that the essential nature of Joseph L. Hudson was shown early in his career, when, as a clothing merchant in Ionia, Michigan (operating a store that his father bought from merchant Christopher R. Mabley), he became "embarrassed" (a contemporary term for bankrupt) during the worldwide financial panic of 1873. Years later, Hudson returned to Detroit to work for Mabley but, after a series of disagreements with his employer and his mercurial (to put it kindly) wife, began his own department store business on the ground floor of the Detroit Opera House on Campus Martius. By 1888, the store had moved onto Woodward Avenue, and Hudson showed his character by doing something unheard of. Before building his dream—the new Big Store on Farmer Street—Hudson repaid, with compound interest, every creditor that had lost money as a result of his 1873 failure. From that moment on, there would be no doubt about the man's character or where his business was going.

The Big Store was indeed built and celebrated its grand opening in 1893 on a very visible site across from the Detroit Public Library on Farmer Street. To gain access to the all-important Woodward Avenue, the store continued to expand bit-by-bit, buying Woodward Avenue lots and building narrow, ten-story tall buildings that connected back to the Big Store until even patrician competitor (and Detroit's oldest department store) Newcomb, Endicott & Co. was purchased and its buildings were demolished for what was called the "Greater Hudson Store." Eventually, the store expanded to practically the whole block, replaced its outdated Big Store and became the retail powerhouse any Detroit competitor had to contend with. The Hudson block, bounded by Woodward Avenue, Grand River Avenue, Farmer Street and Gratiot Avenue was not completed until 1946, when the holdout Sallan block (named after the well-regarded jewelry store that was once located there) on its southwest corner was finally acquired and a matching twelve-story addition put a new and cohesive face on the southern façade of the store.

Crowley's came to be located kitty-corner from Hudson's at the corner of Gratiot Avenue and Farmer Street, making comparison shopping trips between the two stores easy in spite of the fact that Detroit's retail area spread out with the city's unique geometrical street pattern, unlike famous State Street in Chicago or Euclid Avenue in nearby Cleveland, where department store anchors were located on a major urban axis that concentrated retail facilities along its length. Woodward was Detroit's answer to these retail axes, but in Detroit, much was located on the side streets in the downtown cluster as well.

Directly across Gratiot Avenue, south of Hudson's, lay the smallest of Detroit's three major department stores, the Ernst Kern Company, founded on March 13, 1882, at 161 St. Antoine Street at Lafayette Avenue East. The owners were Lutheran immigrants from the province of Württemberg, Germany. Ernst and Maria Held Kern owned the fledgling dry goods store that found success selling lace, trimmings and ribbons to the carriage trade of late nineteenth-century Detroit. After being burned out of the premises in 1886, the Kerns relocated their store to the corner or Randolph Street and Monroe Avenue, where growth of the business led to the purchase of the Finney Hotel building on the southeast corner of Woodward and Gratiot around the turn of the century. On this site, a new five-story building was constructed to house the store's operations. Ernst Kern Sr. passed away in 1901, and his widow and sons, Otto and Ernst C. Kern, oversaw continued growth at the Kern's corner. Maria Kern continued to serve in a managerial capacity for some years after her husband's passing.

The prosperity of pre-Depression Detroit saw Kern's purchase the ten-story Weber building to the east and build a connecting structure over the alley that separated the acquisition from the main store. The big news of the late 1920s was, however, Kern's acquisition of property down Woodward Avenue, all the way to Campus Martius, for a major expansion program. The new store was built in three steps: The first ten-story terra-cotta building

Nearly forgotten, the Ernst Kern Company was an independent retailer housed in a magnificent retail structure. Its destruction in 1966 for urban renewal that didn't happen left a gaping hole in the middle of the city for many years. *From the Manning Brothers Historic Photograph Collection.*

was designed by stalwart Detroit architects Smith, Hinchamn & Grylls in 1920, with the second section following in 1928. The third step involved the demolition of the old five-story store on the corner and its replacement.

When the handsome facility was completed, Kern's had three hundred feet of Woodward Avenue frontage, luxuriously executed in terra cotta details, towering ten stories above Woodward Avenue traffic. A slightly chamfered corner at Gratiot Avenue gently acknowledged the store's giant competitor across the street and lent Kern's new store an elegant continuity of design—reinforced by the Neoclassical style of the façades—which its large neighbor lacked. It could easily be argued that the delicacy, rhythm, order and beauty of the design reflected the similar qualities of its Teutonic owners.

Inside, the store possessed a lofty and palatial main floor promenade, made possible by thirty-foot-high ceilings, which was ringed along the perimeter by a mezzanine level with decorative iron railings enhancing the effect of openness. White-painted chamfered square columns on the main floor rose up to stylized Corinthian capitals supporting a brilliant white ceiling from which delicate Art Deco–influenced chandeliers hung. From the polished white stone floor, richly detailed mahogany wood-and-glass cabinetry extended from dark stone bases and showcased Kern's top-quality merchandise to admiring customers.

Kern's floor area was further augmented in 1937 when Bond Clothiers built a new building at the corner of Woodward and Campus Martius. Bond's let two upper floors and the basement to Kern's for additional sales space. Even though Kern's was roughly one-half the size of Crowley's and only a fraction of Hudson's floor area, the store prospered in Detroit and celebrated its seventy-fifth anniversary in style in 1957. By then it was run by Otto Kern, son of the founder, along with his sons Ernst F. and Richard C. Kern. The installation of a stylish Art Deco clock above the marquee at the corner of Woodward and Gratiot gave Detroit a long-lived and legendary meeting place where once generations of Detroiters admonished their companions to "meet me under Kern's clock."

At the time of the anniversary, Otto Kern told the *Detroit News* that it was

75 years in which downtown Detroit has been in our hearts. We at Kern's have explicit faith and confidence in the continuing importance of Detroit's downtown shopping market as exemplified by the tremendous building and improvement now under way, not only by our beautiful new Civic Center and proposed new seaport [The opening of the St. Lawrence Seaway would soon connect Detroit to the world's markets by ship] *but also by our downtown businesses. In our 75 years in our downtown location, we have served thousands of customers with over a half billion dollars' worth of goods, and we look forward as a family-owned downtown store with optimistic faith in the future.*

Across Woodward Avenue past Hudson's stood the Majestic Building, long ago released from its role as a department store, now with a bank and small retail shops on the street floor. In the same block stood Sanders Confectionery, Detroit's poplar spot for ice cream sundaes and hot-fudge cream puffs or to purchase dainty boxes of the store's "Boulevard" assortment of chocolates. Also on the block, at the corner of State Street, was the flagship store of the B. Siegel Co., a high-fashion shop that replaced the old-line Heyn's Bazaar on the site. Siegel's gave the big department stores a run for their money when it came to high fashion. Later, Hughes & Hatcher, the Detroit-based haberdasher originally located farther north at Woodward and Montcalm (next to the Fox Theater) built a modern, slate-faced flagship store between Siegel's and the seven-story former Parisian Co. building to the south.

Siegel's itself was an up-to-date fashion mecca housed in a six-story building behind an exquisite cast-iron façade. The store was established by Benjamin Siegel after he gained experience working in an old-line store in Detroit known as Heyn's Bazaar. Always considered one of the most exclusive of Detroit's fashion stores, Siegel's sold women's and children's clothing downtown, and its familiar script logo graced a number of large suburban branches in the big shopping centers.

Across State Street, the west side of Woodward held large Kresge and Woolworth stores, catering to bargain hunters and those in search of odds and ends or a light meal at one of their lunch counters. In between, Detroit fashion retailer Kline's occupied an eight-story, three-bay building that converted to City Stores' New York City–based Franklin Simon nameplate in 1958. Chain store Lerner Shops had a presence on this block, too.

Continuing north along Woodward Avenue and across West Grand River Avenue, the buildings of the block were home to the Pittsburgh-based Frank & Seder department store until the company closed its Detroit branch in 1951. Plagued by labor troubles and lacking branch stores that catered to growing suburban areas, the popular-price retailer closed its Detroit and Philadelphia branches until only the Pittsburgh flagship remained, but that, too, closed in 1958. After that time, the block housed a variety of retailers, such as Albert's, Park Lane Hosiery and a number of shoe shops, including Baker's Qualicraft Shoes, Chandler's and Maling's.

Just to the north, an older building housing the established Annis Furs store at 1505 Woodward was replaced by a streamlined gold-and-black porcelain-sheathed structure for the once-ubiquitous Richman Brothers tailoring company. Once topped by an Art Deco spire, the store was covered with neon signage (allowed in the days before signage ordinances) stating:

Richman's Clothes
Style Quality Value
Our Factories to You
No Middleman's Profit
Men's Fine Clothes
Established 1879
The Richman Brothers Co.

The building's fabulous recessed corner entry, detailed in bright aluminum and dark polished stone, housed two-sided vitrines and couldn't have been more of a contrast to its Neoclassical-style next-door neighbor.

The Grinnell Brothers Music House at 1515 Woodward, like its neighbor, the work of Detroit architect Albert Kahn, began in Ann Arbor and eventually came to be the world's largest music store, selling pianos, organs, instruments, sheet music and everything professional or amateur musicians might need. The firm's Holly piano factory was once the world's largest, and the company billed itself as the world's largest distributor of pianos. Its 1908 building, sheathed in gleaming white terra cotta, met the sky with a beautifully molded cornice supported on three delicate jack arches infilled with glass, eventually received a streamlined storefront on its lower levels, paneled in dark stone.

Between these buildings and the towers (from west to east: the Tuller Hotel, the Statler, the David Whitney Building and the Eaton Tower) surrounding Grand Circus Park, like so many exclamation points announcing the semicircular green space, stood Himelhoch Brothers and Company. This regal store was essentially a women's fashion retailer, but due to its size and the fact that it eventually opened a men's shop and offered a limited selection of giftware, competed with Saks Fifth Avenue (located since 1940 in the New Center area of Detroit) and Hudson's Woodward Shops to fill society's desire for high fashion and exclusive goods.

Originally displaced from lower Woodward Avenue by the growth of Hudson's, Himelhoch Brothers and Company advertised its address as "Woodward Avenue through to Washington Boulevard" to publicize its

HIMELHOCH'S

Fashion retailer Himelhoch Brothers and Company was the only major downtown retailer with a presence on both Woodward Avenue and Washington Boulevard. *Collection of the author.*

presence on Detroit's more upscale street as well as on its primary one. The store, founded by Jewish brothers Moses, Israel, Zella and Herman Himelhoch, moved to 1545 Woodward in 1907 and expanded westward with a Washington Boulevard addition that opened in April 1923. While the entrance on the so-called Fifth Avenue of Detroit was eventually given a slick, modern treatment, the presentation inside remained of the highest order. The building featured shops such as the Boutique, the XXI Century Room and the Gold Room in addition to more practical departments like a toy shop for children.

Across the street, the blocks on the other side of Woodward, between Grand Circus Park and Hudson's, housed a number of stores with famous names in retailing, like Wright-Kay & Co. jewelers, A.S. Beck Shoes and Lane Bryant. One of the most interesting of Crowley's competitors were the D.J. Healy shops at 1426 Woodward Avenue. Founded on Saint Patrick's Day 1882 by Daniel J. Healy, a Roman Catholic who immigrated to Detroit from Queenstown (now Cobh), Ireland, in 1862, the store began as a small feather shop (the decorating of hats was of importance in the day's fashion) but eventually grew to carry a full line of women's clothing, men's furnishings, fine arts, furniture and imported Irish linens. Healy's was one of the first Detroit stores to build branch stores in outlying areas of Detroit and its inner suburbs.

New York women's fashion store Russek's occupied the sober six-story-with-attic building next to Healy's, but that store was replaced in 1956 with the familiar Detroit fashion store Winkelman's. The Healy building, after the retailer went out of business in the early '60s, became the site of a Marianne clothing store.

Of course, it is impossible to describe the downtown shopping experience wholly in a book dedicated to one department store. Except for long-term, well-established retailers, the occupancy situation downtown was fluid over the years, and in general, the shops, stores, banks and eateries spread away from Woodward Avenue. Washington Boulevard was known for its airline ticket offices but also served as a high-fashion center with stores like Peck & Peck, E.J. Hickey and Robinson Furniture vying for business with Himelhoch's, which, as mentioned earlier, fronted both Woodward Avenue and the more elegant and leafy Washington Boulevard.

Other stores, like credit retailer People's Outfitting Company, did business on Michigan Avenue. Still others, such as Annis Furs and Fashions or Macaulay's Stationers, helped spread the retail district east along Broadway and Farmer Streets. Away from the avenues and boulevards, retailing was more specialized due to the lower rents on secondary streets. Several branches of Cunningham's and Ligget's drugstores were located on the streets on either side of Woodward. Any mention of Detroit drugstores must include Kinsel's, Detroit's first twenty-four-hour drugstore, located at Michigan and Griswold. Kinsel's, which was folded into the Cunningham chain in 1958, was a day-and-night fixture in the life of Detroit's downtown.

Still farther outside the main Woodward Avenue shopping district, R.H. Fyfe and Co. was perhaps the world's tallest shoe store, occupying as it did a fourteen-story building just north of Grand Circus Park on Woodward. Fyfe's housed over 100,000 pairs of shoes for men, women and children; a putting green (for trying out golf shoes); a foot-care clinic; a shoe repair center; and an auditorium. The buff stone of its tall, narrow headquarters, again the work of Smith, Hinchman & Grylls, was delicately detailed in a Neo-Gothic style that emphasized verticality and drew shoppers' eyes northward like a beacon.

The essential question remains, though: What was it really like, going downtown and shopping at Crowley's? One-time Crowley, Milner & Co. employee Norine Blake of Washington Township remembers her first job downtown. "My mother suggested I go downtown and see what kind of job I could get, right out of high school," she remembered. "Of course, that meant my best dress, heels, a hat and gloves." When asked what seemed most remarkable about her experience, she replied: "The most remarkable thing to me was that Crowley's hired me on the spot. I did pretty well in school, but I was very inexperienced. Before you know it, though, I was working in the seventh-floor offices, and one of my prime responsibilities was to go from department to department collecting time cards. I got to know that store inside and out."

Likewise, Donna Ron, who lives in Israel, remembers her youth in Detroit:

I am happy to write about memories of Crowley's and Detroit. I used to take the Hamilton bus from 7 Mile and Livernois to Hudson's. It was a long ride all through Detroit and I saw everyone. My mother used to like Crowley's because they had cheaper merchandise than Hudson's, which she liked. That was one of our shopping destinations, even though it was not as nice inside as the bigger store was. In 1959 and 1960, I was on the teen modeling panel at Hudson's. I loved it. I had good taste even then, though we didn't have the money to back it up. A few years earlier, when I was 10, I remember wanting a pair of pink buck shoes, and we wound up at Fyfe's, where I got my wish. Something was wrong with them, but Fyfe's stood behind their merchandise, and I can remember my mother writing them a letter of appreciation.

Stephen Kennedy is a former executive of Crowley's. In spite of being a nonagenarian, his memories present a clear view of the store, its operations and its setting. Kennedy's path through life could itself fill a highly entertaining and informative volume, and his story provides a fascinating insight into life in the twentieth century. Born to a single mother in the Baptist South, he was sent north to live with foster families as a small child. "As I got older, I got sick of being shipped from family to family. I had five different surnames, and as soon as I could, I just left. You can't live in a situation where you don't feel loved, and I lived on the streets of New York selling Collier's and newspapers." When asked why he did that, he said: "Simple. I was hungry."

Kennedy's story continues through his service in World War II, where, as a marine (he enlisted at age sixteen in order to "find himself"), he fought in Okinawa and Saipan and was in Nagasaki when the Japanese surrendered and the conflict finally ended. Stateside, he completed two years of high school and sought employment as a drill-press operator but learned that, as a result of the G.I. Bill, he could get a college education. With his last two dollars, he traveled by Greyhound bus to Monmouth, Illinois, to study economics at Monmouth College, where he achieved his degree in economics. In the 1950s, he came to work for Bloomingdale's in New York, where he participated in that store's well-respected executive training program and subsequently became head of the store's statistics department. After later working at Lazarus in Columbus, Ohio, he interviewed for a job in 1964 at Crowley, Milner & Co. in Detroit and worked for the retailer until his retirement in 1989.

Stephen Kennedy   *Norine Blake*

Left: Steven Kennedy, around the time he came to Detroit to Work at Crowley's. *Right*: Norine Blake's high school graduation picture, taken just before her stint at Crowley's. *Courtesy of Steven Kennedy and Norine Blake.*

The experience and recollection that Kennedy has in such abundance provides a great deal of insight into Crowley's, its people and its operations. He speaks of his leadership in revamping the store's archaic credit system and tackling the enormous merchandise loss problem Crowley's suffered in the 1970s as Detroit declined from one of the country's great cities into a crime-ridden skeleton of its former self. His relationships at the store were as wide ranging as his life experience, from Crowley's CEO Robert Winkel to his impressions of typical Crowley employees:

> *Of course, I knew Mrs. Katherine Travis, a granddaughter of the founder; a smart, articulate lady and I loved her to death. Our people were nice folks, usually older, but they cared about their jobs and we cared about them. As a matter of fact, we could count on our people come hell or high water. There was a woman named Sadie who worked in the restaurant, a delightful, beautiful African American lady. Once, I took my sons to "Breakfast with Santa" and they all met her. For years, we couldn't run into each other in the hallway without her saying "Hi, Mr. Kennedy! How are those fine boys of yours doing?"*

Ask Stephen Kennedy what he thought of Detroit and its downtown in 1964 when he came to start work at Crowley's, and you'll get a concise, sincere and accurate reply. "When I got out of the cab, I remember thinking: I have never seen so many babushkas in my whole life!"

3

PARDRIDGE IN A PEAR TREE

*U*nlike many famous department stores, Crowley, Milner & Co. did not begin as a tiny enterprise that grew into a massive metropolitan department store, much as a caterpillar metamorphoses into a brilliantly colored butterfly. Crowley's, in its own unique way, was born of the unfortunate failure of a bright light in Detroit's retail arena, the firm of Pardridge & Blackwell. One of Detroit's largest department store firms, Pardridge & Blackwell christened itself the "Heart of Detroit" and in many ways it was just that in the early part of the twentieth century. In fact, this all-but-forgotten department store's evolution forms the basis for Crowley, Milner & Co.'s own history. It is a twisting, turning story of success and failure, with a little murder and intrigue thrown in for good measure.

Even before Pardridge & Blackwell, there was Pardridge & Walsh, and before that, the story has its beginnings in Chicago, where Edwin Pardridge perfected a method of short-selling grain futures and was hailed as "the heaviest bear speculator the Chicago Board of Trade has ever known" by the *Chicago Tribune* in 1896.

Before this well-known and respected "plunger" honed his trading methods, he mastered the retail business. Born on October 24, 1835, near Durhamville, New York, Edwin Pardridge served his apprenticeship at a local general store until eventually moving to Lyons, New York. From there, Pardridge relocated to Chicago, where he opened a store on the corner of State and Lake Streets with his brother, Charles W. Pardridge. In spite of being burnt out in the great Chicago Fire of 1871, the store prospered and relocated to 118–24 State Street, where it became known as "the Boston Store." By 1876, Pardridge and his brother had an active partner in the person of Charles Netcher, who oversaw the store's expansion and acquisition of branch stores in Buffalo and Detroit.

The *Chicago Tribune*, in its obituary of Edwin Pardridge that appeared on April 18, 1896, commented on the businessman's retail policies:

> *He came* [to Chicago], *he said, for a larger field of operations than he had had, and in the conduct of his store, he shared the same discriminating judgement and mastery of details as applied to the buying and selling of goods that applied on his grain operations on the Board of Trade.*

During this time, Edwin Pardridge interested himself in speculation and became active in grain trading. He invested heavily in real estate as a hedge against the significant potential for losses in his risky new venture. He entrusted his real estate affairs in Chicago to his agent, Robert J. Walsh, who had come from Ireland at the age of fourteen and in 1864 and worked first as an office boy for Pardridge. While Edwin Pardridge became fabulously wealthy as a result of his grain trading activities and eventually lost interest in the retail trade, Walsh grew to become a trusted associate.

Edwin Pardridge's Detroit store, Pardridge & Co., was founded on Monroe Avenue in 1871, the same year his son Willard was born. In 1896, just before his death due to kidney disease, Edwin Pardridge was actively disposing of his retail interests. After the elder Pardridge's demise, twenty-five-year-old Willard, along with Robert J. Walsh, bought the Detroit store, and the firm of Pardridge & Walsh ("The People's Dry Goods Trading Emporium") was established in the growing city on the banks of the Detroit River.

Pardridge, characterized by the *Detroit Free Press* as "a hustling young merchant," became known as the youngest retailer on Woodward Avenue. The city took note as his store prospered and became thronged with customers. The newspaper described the young man just after the turn of the century, saying:

> *As unassuming as the humblest employee, his identity would deceive the keenest observer. A short acquaintance with Mr. Pardridge, however, convinces one that he possesses in a marked degree the qualities that command success. This young man has early reaped the rewards of patient merit, untiring industry and steady application to business. It is simply another illustration of the fact that a wise head is often set on young shoulders.*

Pardridge & Walsh did a booming business in the late 1800s from this small building on the southwest corner of Woodward Avenue at Congress Street. *Collection of the author.*

By the time Willard Pardridge took ownership of the former Pardridge & Co., it had moved to Woodward Avenue, the all-important spine of Detroit that stretched from the docks of the Detroit River, on the southwest corner of Congress Street. The store, with four floors and a basement, was situated in a typical brick commercial building with a massive wood cornice surmounted by a pediment at the center of its Woodward façade.

The *Detroit Free Press* described the store's remodel, which took place shortly after Willard Pardridge took control (Robert J. Walsh being a more or less silent partner who spent most of his time in Chicago looking after his considerable real estate holdings), saying that:

Among all the improvements in various Woodward Avenue business blocks of late there has been none more conspicuous for its sustainability and practical marks of progress than that of the dry goods house of Pardridge & Walsh, corner of Woodward Avenue and Congress Street. Careful planning and liberality in expenditures have contributed to make the remodeled store one of the most imposing in that busy street, and the firm are to be congratulated upon the success of their efforts to keep the mercantile tone up to a metropolitan standard.

The article, entitled "Credit to Woodward Ave.," also stated that "the front has been entirely changed and presents an attractive and inviting appearance in its artistically simple details" and that "the interior of the building is thoroughly in keeping with the exterior, no pains having been spared to make it wholly modern both in appearance and equipment." Elsewhere, the *Free Press* extolled the "latest improvements" in store fixtures installed by Pardridge & Walsh and speculated upon the increased convenience and ultimate satisfaction these features would offer the store's customers.

Hyperbole aside, Pardridge & Walsh may have gone the way of many enterprising but short-lived retailers in those heady days of Detroit's growth. However, a tragic event conspired to change the future for the enterprise. Back in Chicago, on February 21, 1899, Robert J. Walsh was confronted outside of his office in the Roanoke Building by Daniel Driscoll, whom the *Detroit Free Press* described as "said to have been drinking and was quarrelsome." After a brief confrontation, Driscoll fatally shot Walsh five times at close range, saying, when the police arrived, "I have just killed Bob Walsh. I killed him and that is all I have to say."

Later, according to the *Chicago Tribune*, Driscoll explained that he killed the thirty-five-year old because the businessman had released him from his job as janitor of a building Walsh owned on the previous day. He also stated that his actions were aggravated by the amount of abuse he took from his employer and that when being dismissed, Walsh referred to him as "a cur" and "a worthless rascal."

The murder was certainly a tragedy, but its byproduct was a change in direction for the Detroit dry goods store. Henry Blackwell, a native of Limerick, Ireland, had completed an extensive dry goods apprenticeship in the city of his birth and eventually came to the United States in 1892 as a thirty-one-year-old. By chance, he met James S. Chawke, the general manager of Pardridge & Walsh, shortly after his arrival in New York City. The two men had been friends back on the Auld Sod, and Chawke, knowing of Blackwell's experience and business acumen, encouraged the younger man to move to Detroit and take a position with his Woodward Avenue employer.

Blackwell agreed and started with Pardridge & Walsh as a floor walker but, in a few years, was elevated to manager of the store's second floor, which housed the company's offerings of millinery, cloaks, ready-to-wear garments and shoes. After instituting practices that tripled the business of his floor in just one year, Pardridge was made general manager of the store on June 1, 1898, shortly before Robert J. Walsh's murder in Chicago. Indeed, it was Henry Blackwell who received the telegram on that fateful day in February 1899 from Willard Pardridge, who was also in Chicago looking after his late father's estate matters and remaining business interests. Pardridge told Blackwell: "R.J. Walsh was shot this morning and died instantly. Let business go on as usual until further notice."

The increase in Pardridge & Walsh's business during the time of Blackwell's management was such that the store eventually needed to expand. The old location at Woodward and Congress was reportedly "thronged" with customers, never more so than during the mill-end sales, in which the store partnered with C.A. Lockhart, a flamboyant mill agent, to bring bargain-priced merchandise into the store for a semiannual, weeklong sale event. The local newspapers reported that the mill-end sale of March 1899 "taxed the capacity of Pardridge & Walsh's store. In addition, the *Detroit Free Press* reported the scene on the second day of the sale, saying:

> *The clerks at Pardridge & Walsh's have had a busy time of it for the past two days, and there is every indication that they will have their hands full for the balance of this week. Monday was the opening of the mill-end sale now in progress, and so great was the crush of those in search of bargains that several times during the day the management found it necessary to close the doors to others desiring to enter, until the crowd inside could be in a measure thinned out. Yesterday, there was no apparent decrease in the throng of purchasers, notwithstanding the chilly blasts that swept through the streets.*

It was Henry Blackwell who engineered a move to larger premises, but to understand how the growing firm's expansion was accomplished, it is necessary to have knowledge of the position the store known as Mabley & Company held in the Detroit retail scene at the turn of the century. It was the spectacular failure of Mabley's after its founder's death that paved the way for Henry Blackwell to take Pardridge & Walsh on to bigger and better things.

Among Detroit's favored retail stores in the late nineteenth century was the house of Christopher R. Mabley on Woodward Avenue just south of the Campus Martius. The merchant, born in St. Minver, Cornwall, England, in 1836, received his training from age eleven in the tailoring department of his father's local establishment. When the family immigrated to Canada, he masterminded the establishment of a clothing store there as a young man. He made his way to Milwaukee, Wisconsin, two years after opening another family store in London, Ontario. The Milwaukee venture, while successful, was the victim of a fire, after which Mabley moved east and settled in Pontiac, Michigan, in 1859. Recognizing that greater opportunity lay to the south in Detroit, he opened a small clothing store at 126 Woodward Avenue, in the same block as the city's *soigné* Russell House Hotel, on his birthday in February 1870.

In the following years, Mabley's success was such that the store grew from its original two-floor twenty- by one-hundred-foot space into a gargantuan (for the day) retail complex extending down the block and even across the street in two separate buildings. It was generally agreed at the time that Mabley's success was not just due to his innate understanding of the retail trade and mastery of the ready-made clothing business but also to the two signs he pasted on the storefront on his first day in business, stating "One Price Only" and "Terms Strictly Cash." Like many well-known merchants, Mabley did not invent these policies, but he did envision the increase in business and profit their implementation could provide. His dedication was not without doubt and challenge, as the *Detroit Free Press* related five years after his death:

> It is no wonder that Mr. Mabley had a hard row to hoe when he launched out and proclaimed his business principles. Customers were accustomed in those days not to buy anything until after they had "Jewed" the dealer out of all his profits—as they often imagined. Credit was universal and many "solid" citizens left Mr. Mabley's store indignant because it was denied them, and found solace in predicting Mabley's speedy downfall. It was then that the trade reformer had a hard struggle to keep his head above the surface. It is said that the success of the experiment turned on the sale of a $12 suit for which a customer said he would only pay $10. Mr. Mabley explained that it was his policy to sell cheap for cash, and

Mabley & Company was housed in a large structure on the east side of Woodward Avenue. When Mabley's left, the building became the Metropole Hotel and still stands, rather brutalized by time, in its original location. *Courtesy of the Detroit Public Library.*

that he had only one price. "That sounds well enough," said the customer as he turned away, "but it is my policy never to pay the price asked for anything." "Maybe I am wrong," thought Mr. Mabley, "and all the others are right. Perhaps I had better give in." While he was still debating on the proposition the customer unexpectedly returned and took the suit at the price asked, saying that nowhere in Detroit could it be bought so cheap. "That settled it," ejaculated Mr. Mabley, "this will remain a one-price house."

It is amusing to note that one of Mabley's most respected employees was none other than J.L. Hudson, who himself founded a great retail establishment, but the story of the two men's relationship could fill a book on its own. A feud ensued between them after Mabley's meddlesome wife scolded Hudson for following Mabley's orders to erect a sign beside the Mableys' home advertising the store to state fairgoers while Mabley was on a buying trip to Europe. The disagreement turned in to a veritable battle royale between the three upon the store owner's return.

The aftermath saw Hudson leave Mabley's employ to establish his own men's clothing business in retail space on the ground floor of the Detroit

Opera House that had just been vacated (for larger quarters on Woodward Avenue) by one of Detroit's most august dry goods firms, Newcomb, Endicott & Co. The changing and variable nature of early retailing in Detroit is illustrated by the fact that, forty-five years later, Hudson's enormous Woodward Avenue establishment would devour even Newcomb, Endicott & Co.'s large store on the same block, laying to rest Newcomb's run as Detroit's first and oldest department store.

The Hudson/Mabley feud that resulted from the split saw the institution of "sacrifice" sales, with one competitor attempting to outdo the other, and reckless competition that resulted in mobbed stores and the respective business owners returning home for little more than occasional catnaps during the business week.

Christopher R. Mabley died after a brief illness in June 1885, aged forty-nine. He was about to leave on another trip to Europe, intending this time to recuperate and regain his health. Owing to the fact that he had operated, with various partners, retail stores in Cincinnati (the noted Mabley & Carew), Louisville, Baltimore and Cleveland, among others, his passing was mourned regionally if not nationally.

Mabley & Company in Detroit was reorganized after its founder's demise and was left in the hands of his former associate Bruce Goodfellow, who himself came from Canada (via Toronto) to settle in Detroit and take up a career in retailing. Beginning as a clerk in 1875, Goodfellow rose through the organization until he became secretary and treasurer just before Christopher R. Mabley's death, after which time he succeeded his employer as president of the store.

One of Mabley's dreams was to erect a fitting monument to his organization in Detroit, and Goodfellow concentrated on this goal after Mabley died. By November 11, 1892, suitable property at the corner of Woodward and Michigan Avenues was fully acquired, and Goodfellow announced, according to the *Detroit Free Press*, that Mabley & Company would build "the most pretentious structure in the city, in keeping with the prominence of the corner on which it is to be erected." At this early date, an eight-story retail store, not quite as tall as the much-celebrated and new Hammond block on the other side of Detroit's old City Hall, was envisioned. By June 1895, when the ultimate design, by D.H. Burnham of Chicago (noted architect of the 1893 World's Columbian Exposition), was revealed in a newspaper illustration, the building had grown to a fourteen-story skyscraper that included six floors of leasable office space above Mabley's projected new store.

An early illustration of the Mabley building as planned. The new name, Majestic Building, allowed the many letter *M*s that adorned the building, executed in terra cotta and brass, to remain in place and still have relevance. *Collection of the author.*

The desired pretentiousness was to be achieved by richly detailed façades of colored terra cotta, crowned with an observation deck that was in reality a fifteenth floor. Giant, two-story archways promised a "very lofty and imposing effect" in combination with the building's projecting stone balconies above the second-floor level and a variegated composition of roman-arched and flat-top windows below the deep cornice that was to overhang the sidewalk where the building met the sky. Interior appointments, the paper reported, were to be finished in "marble and hardwoods" and incorporate "a spacious gallery devoted to a luxurious reception room for visitors [and] the private offices of Bruce Goodfellow…and the cashier and bookkeepers." It would be the tallest building built in Michigan up to that time.

Yet all of this splendor was planned in the midst of the Panic of 1893, the worst depression the country had known until that time. Banks, railroads and businesses failed at an alarming rate, and unemployment in Michigan soared to 43 percent. Mabley's and the consortium put together to build Goodfellow's skyscraper monument to the store's founder was in deep trouble. When, by April 1896, it looked as though the building's developers would go bankrupt and leave Detroit with an unfinished white elephant, the *Detroit Free Press* literally begged the city's businessmen to step up and guarantee the Mabley Building's completion.

Even worse for Mabley & Company, the store had placed a stunning amount of merchandise on order in anticipation of larger quarters and was forced to sell the stock at markdowns from its old premises. As a result of the delays and problems, Mabley & Company descended into a financial chaos and entered into receivership. The *Detroit Free Press* of November 24, 1896, opined:

> *One will look in vain for any element of retributive justice in the financial reverses that have overtaken the long-established and thoroughly known firm of Mabley & Company. Enterprising, tireless, resourceful and efficiently officered and managed, nothing but the protracted depression which has enforced retrenchment upon every consumer and caused creditors to become exacting and insistent could have forced this popular house upon the commercial shoals.*

By this time, Mabley's had closed both its bazaar and shoe store buildings across the street and moved out its leased premises on the ground floor of the adjacent Russell House hotel. Before the end of the year, however, it was announced that the remaining assets of Mabley & Company were sold to W.S.

Peck & Co. of Syracuse, New York. The resultant new firm was to be known as Mabley & Goodfellow, and when it opened to great fanfare on April 15, 1897, in the newly renamed Majestic Building, the future seemed bright indeed. By February of the next year, though, Mabley & Goodfellow was out of business, the Majestic Building filed suit for rent it was owed and the agonizing death of the Mabley store in Detroit had practically come to its conclusion.

For a while, another Syracuse merchant arrived on the scene to operate the store, but Charles A. Shafer was every bit as unsuccessful as his predecessors, even as the economy improved and the depression spawned by the Panic of 1893 became a thing of the past. Shafer did manage to conduct business while fighting a lawsuit brought by the Majestic Building against the store until a major announcement appeared in the press in October 1901.

Throughout the whole convoluted Mabley affair, Pardridge & Walsh continued to operate under Henry Blackwell's leadership and to weather the economic troubles, in spite of the murder of Robert J. Walsh in Chicago. The store's aforementioned 1899 remodeling and well-attended sales events contrasted with the dramatic turns and ultimate failure that dragged Mabley & Company into the retail graveyard. In October 1901, it was announced that Pardridge & Walsh had purchased the stock of C.A. Shafer and concluded a deal with the Majestic Building management to lease four of the eight floors occupied by the predecessor firm for a term of five years.

The deal that would put Pardridge & Walsh in the Majestic Building had been negotiated successfully by Henry Blackwell, and as a reward for his service, he was taken into partnership. It was later announced that, once the old stocks were sold and the store reconfigured, the old premises at Woodward and Congress would be vacated and the reconfigured store on the corner of Woodward and Michigan Avenues would close and ultimately reopen in March 1902 under a new name—Pardridge & Blackwell, "The People's Store."

An interesting historical fact of the Majestic Building's Pardridge & Blackwell era is that illusionist and escape artist Harry Houdini, long before he died in Detroit in 1926, performed at Detroit's Temple Theater on November 24, 1905. The feat that amazed the standing room only crowd was his escape from a packing box he asked employees of Pardridge & Blackwell's shipping department to build, and later secure on stage, with the so-called handcuff king inside. The *Free Press* wrote on the next day that "the sides and bottom and top were nailed so tightly that it was even betting that Sandow (a pioneering German-born body builder) could not break his way out" and that "the box was then roped round and round, criss-cross and

The new store in the Majestic Building was fêted with an elaborate grand opening celebration. Photos of the event would be rare in any case, but this illustration shows the crowds and the balcony that housed the store management's offices. *Collection of the author.*

every way and nails driven into the ropes." The paper reported that the crowd waited anxiously for nine minutes until Houdini emerged from the box and "a great shout went up." Theatergoers stormed the stage to shake the magician's hand, calling him a "peach" and proclaiming him "the greatest ever." The article did not record the crowd's comments on the Pardridge & Blackwell employees who failed to foil the artistry of the crowd's hero whose escape carried the day.

During this time, a family of Irish descent and professing the Roman Catholic faith began their own rise to fame in the world of Detroit's business interests. Cornelius Crowley (1822–1895) and his wife, Catherine (Bresnahan) Crowley (1833–1901), came to settle in Detroit's Corktown district after arriving in North America in 1850. Crowley was a grocer and owned a neighborhood store at 91 Porter Street, a stone's throw from his place of worship, Most Holy Trinity Roman Catholic church, the de facto center of the burgeoning Irish American neighborhood. Interestingly, Most Holy Trinity church was founded in 1834 under the administration of twenty-three-year-old Father Martin Kundig, a former Swiss Guard at the Vatican who studied in Rome in preparation for a missionary career in the New World.

Above, left to right: Historic portraits of William L. Milner (1838–1922) and Joseph J. Crowley (1862–1925); *Below, left to right*: William C. Crowley (1886–1927) and Daniel T. Crowley (1864–1936). *Courtesy of Michael Hauser.*

The Crowleys' marriage produced three sons—Joseph Jeremiah (1862–1925), Daniel Thomas (1864–1936) and William Cornelius (1866–1927), who all received education at Trinity School. Their parents' grocery operation in the neighborhood apparently exposed them to commerce firsthand, for they all excelled in business, and while Joseph Crowley attended the Detroit Business University, William attended the Jesuit

University of Detroit on the corner of Jefferson Avenue and St. Antoine Street in Detroit.

A biography of Joseph Crowley found in a volume entitled *The City of Detroit 1701–1722* says that, as a clerk at the Detroit wholesale dry goods firm

103-105-107-109-111-113 JEFFERSON AVE. COR. SHELBY ST.

CROWLEY BROTHERS INC.
WHOLESALE DRY GOODS

The Crowley Brothers wholesale dry goods business occupied a site at Jefferson Avenue and Shelby Street, roughly the location of the modern Hotel Pontchartrain. The illustration dates from the day when Detroit's historic riverfront was an intact environment of historical industrial buildings. *Courtesy of the Detroit Public Library.*

of James K. Burnham & Company, where he began working in 1878, the young Crowley recognized that "success slips away from the sluggard, plays as a will-o'-the-wisp before the dreamer but yields its rewards to the man of energy and determination." He worked alongside Frederick R. Stoepel, a German-born immigrant, and when the firm became known as Burnham, Stoepel & Company in 1895, Crowley was offered a partnership, which he duly accepted. Joseph Crowley's brother Daniel worked at the firm from 1880, and William worked there from 1887. Daniel Crowley left the employ of J.K. Burnham & Company in 1886 for a position with the Peninsular Stove Company, where he eventually became vice-president and general manager in 1920.

In November 1901, it was announced in the *Detroit Free Press* that Joseph Crowley would retire on December 1 from Burnham, Stoepel & Company, concurrent with its reorganization into two firms, one in Kansas City owned by James Burnham and the other in Detroit led by Stoepel. The article hinted that Crowley and his brother William would form their own wholesale dry goods house with a "capital of from $300,000 to $400,000." A few weeks later, the *Free Press* let the cat out of the bag by announcing the "New Crowley Brothers Dry Goods Jobbing House" and confirmed that the new company had secured a four-story headquarters building at Jefferson Avenue and Shelby Street in Detroit and that a catalogue would soon be issued. A number of former Burnham, Stoepel & Company employees had been hired by the Crowleys as department heads, and those salesmen had been taken on to spread their wholesale business throughout Michigan and into Ohio and Indiana.

One year later, a brief announcement in the *Free Press* mentioned that the Crowley brothers were contracting for an addition to their headquarters and had acquired adjacent properties. Later, in 1903, the company had acquired even more space and spanned six properties (nos. 103, 105, 107, 109, 111 and 113) along Jefferson Avenue, and its traveling sales staff exceeded twenty persons, while its original selection of dry goods, notions and furnishings had been increased to offer retailers impressive stocks of underwear, hosiery, sweaters, blankets, flannels, dress goods, linoleum and oil cloths.

Unbeknownst to everyone involved, the pieces of the jigsaw puzzle that paved the way for the foundation of Crowley, Milner & Co. were being placed on the table and fitted together most carefully. One of Crowley Brothers' wholesale customers to the south was the great Toledo department store of William L. Milner, called the largest such store between Chicago and Cleveland, and before long, his piece of the puzzle would come into play as well.

4

THE HEART OF DETROIT

*T*he People's Store," as Pardridge & Blackwell liked to call itself, brought traffic and success to the Majestic Building, hosting spring and fall "openings" that drew crowds, as well as continuing C.A. Lockhart's regular mill-end sales for bargain hunters. The two-page ad announcing the spring 1904 mill-end sale also introduced something new—a graphic border consisting of heart-shapes with an image of the Pardridge & Blackwell store, surmounted by the slogan the "Heart of Detroit." This new moniker was clearly in relation to the establishment of the store as a popular fixture right in the center of town.

In March 1905, Pardridge & Blackwell expanded its offerings to include a private bank located on the store's mezzanine. The bank encouraged savings by store patrons and featured an interesting deposit method—customers were provided with a small strong-box that could be taken home, facilitating collection of small change or bills, and then returned to the store to complete the deposit process. Established in conjunction with a New York bank that had already opened several department store banks across the country, the process, Pardridge & Blackwell indicated, was in demand in its store at the time, and the company wished to expand the services offered to its customers.

Success, economic prosperity and a need for space confronted Pardridge & Blackwell's business and made a new home a necessity if the firm were to compete with Joseph L. Hudson's growing enterprise over on Farmer Street. On March 10, 1905, just three years after settling into the Majestic Building, Pardridge & Blackwell announced that it would move to a new structure on Farmer Street between Gratiot and Monroe Avenues. Furthermore, the store would be six stories tall and equipped not only with eight elevators but also with an innovation recently installed "in the department store of R.H. Macy & Co. in New York City"—a moving staircase that allowed customers to travel easily from floor to floor without ever climbing a step.

At a meeting of the Detroit Common Council Committee on Roads and Alleys held to discuss the required closure of a mid-block alley in order to accommodate construction of the store, planned to give Pardridge & Blackwell more than double its current space, many prominent Detroit merchants made their presence known in support of the venture. The committee decided to send a positive report to the Detroit Common Council approving the alley's vacation. The *Detroit Free Press* reported:

> *Messrs. Field, Hinchman & Smith are the architects who designed the building. It will be 220 feet in depth and 100 feet wide. And while it is not a sky scraper as far as the number of stories go, the ceilings will be so high that the structure will be an imposing one. The front will be one unbroken line of plate glass…when Pardridge & Blackwell move into* [the new building]*, the Majestic Building above the ground floor will be devoted entirely to offices. It is probable that the Majestic Building Co. will convert the lower part of the building into an arcade, with quarters for a bank on the corner.*

When further details emerged in the coming days, the new store was not just proclaimed as a momentous addition to the city's business community but also as a harbinger of the growth and betterment of Detroit and an example of the expansion of its shopping district beyond Woodward Avenue, heralding the day when Detroit no longer had to "suffer the reproach of being a one-street town."

When details of the store's design and construction were revealed a few months later, it seemed as if all Detroit was eager to hear about the great building that would transform a block of ancient two-story buildings housing marginal businesses into a modern shopping center. The *Detroit Free Press* opined that the off-the-beaten-track location would serve the city well, explaining that Woodward Avenue could always attract business, but the location of Pardridge & Blackwell's store would reenergize a part of the city that longed for pedestrian traffic. Regarding vehicles, the paper noted, the placement on Gratiot Avenue, one of the city's major arteries, would not force the store to "attract patronage around the corner" because of the bus and streetcar lines traversing the store's perimeter.

After solving the problems of acquiring land and procuring financing, Pardridge & Blackwell announced its move to a new location on Gratiot Avenue and this imposing new retail structure. *Courtesy of Michael Hauser.*

About the building itself, lavish praise was showered on the excitingly new escalator that would connect the first two floors, the provision of five twenty-foot-wide aisles running the length of the building and the mezzanine along the interior of its blank east wall. The provision of a mezzanine (the future location of the firm's in-house bank) was made possible by the soaring, eighteen-foot-high ceiling of the first floor, a novelty that would break from the past, when stores had occupied cramped, ill-lit and low-ceilinged spaces in much smaller buildings. The *Free Press* singled out the "ornamental bronze and glass marquise extending over the sidewalk" and noted that the example at the Gratiot Avenue entrance would extend to the curb and provide Detroit with another first: a covered carriage entrance. The paper continued:

> *One can imagine the beauty of the Farmer Street side of the structure when it is stated that the corners will be immense granite piers and the entrance will be entirely of glass, forming magnificent show windows ninety-five feet in length, free from any break or obstruction. Of the entrances, which, by the way merit a lengthy description, it may be said that they have been so designed that each will be a distinctive feature of the building.*

Among the technical innovations of the new Pardridge & Blackwell facility, it was reported that there would be four passenger elevators and an equal number of freight elevators, all electrically operated. A "gravity package conveyor" chute allowed packages to travel quickly from the sales floor to the store's basement-level shipping room to be shipped to eager customers both near and far away. The building would be supported and protected (from fire) by a steel frame encased in concrete, an innovation of the Chicago School of architecture that was becoming popular due to the many advantages the construction method offered.

As the completion date neared (and after two ironworkers had fallen from the building as its frame rose from Detroit's muddy ground), the genesis of the colossal project became known. Henry Blackwell happened to be on a train to the 1904 Louisiana Purchase Exposition in St. Louis (of *Meet Me in St. Louis* fame) when he encountered J.A. Burns, the Detroit agent for Brown, Durell & Co., a large Boston wholesale dry goods firm. Burns suggested it was time for Pardridge & Blackwell to build a new flagship store on the Farmer Street site, and the proposition intrigued Blackwell, who requested that Burns consult with a legal firm that was capable of assembling the property on the store's behalf. Upon returning to Detroit, Burns contacted the law firm of Arthur C. and John O'Connor, Detroit real estate law specialists who went to work assembling the property on which Pardridge & Blackwell's new store would rise.

They had their work cut out for them. One property was owned by a gentleman, referred to by the *Free Press* as a "hopeless paralytic," with whom negotiations were nearly impossible. The properties owned by several estates were acquired through bargaining by the O'Connors, but another obstacle presented itself in the form of the heirs of several estates who lived as far away as the Philippines, Bermuda and the Isle of Wight on the south coast of England. This being an age of slow communication compared to the present, months were consumed in back-and-forth haggling by mail. The O'Connors were also faced with the unwillingness to move by the lessees of the crinkum-crankum structures on the property, some of whose lease terms extended beyond the construction start date.

Once these real estate matters were out of the way, the requisite financing was sought, and again, it was J.A. Burns's influence that helped Pardridge & Blackwell. The Boston native was able to use his (and his employer's) East Coast connections to secure financing from Bostonians Laurence Minot and Moses Williams, who, according to the *Free Press*, were "members of old and wealthy Boston families, and heads of several large real estate trusts which have large investments in outside cities" owing to the endorsement of many of Pardridge & Blackwell's business partners and vendors.

As the store approached completion in the autumn of 1906, the scaffolding came down and the brilliant composition of the building, executed in a richly detailed Neo-Renaissance style, became apparent to the public. Gleaming white in glazed brick trimmed with white terra cotta, the building had deep shadows from its lavish keystones, corbels, cartouches and rustications that helped bring the rich façades to life. The whole building was capped with a dramatic overhanging cornice supported by countless elaborate scroll brackets, some of which sported carved floral garlands.

At the time of the new Pardridge & Blackwell's completion, it was boasted that eighty thousand glazed bricks were used in its construction, and some of the elaborate glazed terra-cotta pieces weighed as much as one ton each. Five hundred tons of ornamental plaster was used on the interior, primarily as wall surfacing, but also as decorative details, including column capitals on the various floors. Another prominent feature of the interior was the mahogany-toned paneling and casework that added richness and a traditional atmosphere to the interior. The innovative escalators were also clad in wood paneling, and the whole place was kept clean and as dust-free as possible by a centralized vacuum cleaning system, a true innovation in 1907, when the technology was in its infancy, and ages before the public had ever heard of Hoovers, Orecks or Dysons.

The actual opening, originally predicted for a date after the New Year holiday, was a non-event because Pardridge & Blackwell was able to press three floors of the new building into service during the extraordinary crush of shoppers that descended upon downtown Detroit during the 1907 Christmas season. One of Pardridge & Blackwell's holiday ads proclaimed:

> *Good news for our thousands of customers, what a relief to be able to do Christmas shopping at Pardridge & Blackwell's without having to force your way through dense crowds. We never had nearly enough room for December business in the old store; couldn't possibly serve all the customers who wanted to trade with us. This year conditions were worse on account of stocks being the largest we ever provided for the season because more people realize the advantage of trading here. "More space" was the cry of the department managers, and to meet the demand, and also out of consideration for the comfort and convenience of our patrons, we have arranged to use three floors of our new building as well as our present quarters for holiday trade.*

The *Free Press* reported that the store would close after the holidays to allow contractors to complete work on the other floors and that it would replace the old premises once a proper grand opening could be held. The store duly announced a gala grand opening on February 2, 1907, promising both afternoon and evening concerts by Finzel's Full Orchestra, to include Amilcare's popular "Dance of the Hours" (known as "Hello Muddah, Hello Faddah" to the baby boomer generation), excerpts from *Carmen* by Georges Bizet and "Polish Dance" (by now-forgotten composer Oskar Scharwenka), along with lighter fare, including a march entitled "Paddy Whack" (by an even more forgotten Mr. Lampe). About the attractions for the curious and the shopaholics of the day, Pardridge & Blackwell advertised:

> *This invitation is as broad as the policy of this house and is extended to everybody with a hearty good will. We trust it will be accepted by all as a personal expression of welcome. Although service will be ready for those who request it, our special desire is that the public spend the time in viewing the magnificent surroundings and our wonderful exhibition of merchandise. The store will be in gala attire and the display will be worth coming miles and miles to see.*

Come the public did, for the newspapers reported that a throng of 100,000 people explored the wonders of the store the *Free Press* called "a proud example of down-town architecture, solid, well proportioned, clean cut, imposing—a perfect adaptation of means to end." It also pronounced the displays housed in the unbroken line of first-floor windows around all three sides of the building "gorgeous," singled out the stunning displays of Pardridge & Blackwell's design and display director John W. Cameron (including an artistic show case that held 2,500 umbrellas) and mentioned that "if the flowers sent to Messrs. Pardridge and Blackwell yesterday with expressions of friendship from individuals and firms at home and abroad could be gathered into one mass they would form a display in themselves worth going a long distance to see."

The next day, Pardridge & Blackwell took out a full-page ad in the Detroit papers, thanking the crowds of well-wishers and pointing out, by way of a diagram, that "our new home (The Heart of Detroit) is but a few steps away from our old store in the Majestic Building." Elsewhere, the store reminded customers: "You can't mistake the building; it's the handsomest business block in Detroit, besides being one of the finest retail establishments in the United States. Everybody says so."

Pardridge & Blackwell's store was new and innovative when opened. Still, the store leased the ground floor of an adjacent pool hall to accommodate the men's department's need for space, as can be seen to the right of the gleaming white building. *Courtesy of the Library of Congress.*

In July 1907, Pardridge & Blackwell began what would become a long history of food service on the site by opening the "Japanese Café" in the basement of the new store. The room, designed to appeal to the female shopping crowd, was separated from other departments by Asian screens, while colorful Japanese parasols and illuminated lanterns hung from the ceiling, causing the *Free Press* to predict that the "coziness and comfort, the convenience and proximity to all theaters of the pretty place situated in the 'Heart of Detroit' cannot fail but make it one of the most popular spots in the city."

In the same way, it would have seemed at the time, that Pardridge & Blackwell had scored a stunning coup with the attractions and location of its great store and that, in spite of Joseph L. Hudson's prosperity or the inroads gained on Woodward Avenue by the Ernst Kern Company, Pardridge & Blackwell really had become the Heart of Detroit and would remain so, destined to prosper for many years to come. Or would it?

5

RESCUE MISSION

*H*indsight is twenty/twenty, they say. Given the successful history of Pardridge & Blackwell up until 1907 and the store's prestigious new quarters in a prosperous and growing metropolitan area at the very center of an up-and-coming manufacturing segment, the store's management could be forgiven for thinking the future was assured. Perhaps the success even distracted them from the economic calamity that was looming just over the horizon and came to be known as the Panic of 1907.

A number of events throughout the year gave cause to the crisis, which, because it involved primarily the stock market and banks, was referred to as the "rich man's panic." In fact, the government, without much in the way of tools in place to mitigate the collapse of the stock market at the time or the run on banks that characterized the panic, turned to J.P. Morgan, one of its wealthiest citizens, to intervene by infusing money from his personal fortune into collapsing banks. As a result, the event was short-lived but intense, far-reaching and of great consequence for Pardridge & Blackwell.

The year 1907 was characterized in business and financial circles as one of market instability, with new legislation in effect causing the crash of a number of key stocks, including the Union Pacific Railroad as a result of the new rate-setting powers of the Interstate Commerce Commission and Standard Oil due to recently enacted antitrust laws. In addition, the United States' money supply was compromised by an increase in interest rates by the Bank of England, causing cash to flow eastbound across the Atlantic and making the country cash poor without any kind of central bank to protect it.

This was all just the background to an event that would shortly bring many banks to their knees.

F. Augustus Heinze, who had made a fortune in Montana's copper industry, along with his brother Otto and "robber baron" banker Charles F. Morse, devised a scheme to corner the market on the stock of the United Copper Company. Otto's plan was to corner "short-sellers" of the stock of his brother's United Copper Company by driving up the price of stock, making them unable to replace the stock they "borrowed" to sell at a high price and buy back profitably at a reduced rate. New York's Knickerbocker Trust Company financed the Heinze's stock-buying spree, and the price of United Copper's shares rose from thirty-nine dollars to as high as sixty-two dollars, but when the short-sellers found low-cost stock to replace the amount (desperately smaller than Otto's estimates) they borrowed, the stock fell to fifteen dollars per share, and it was the Heinzes and their conspirators who were themselves ruined.

To everyone's horror, Augustus Heinze had invested his fortune in, and gained control of, twenty-five different state and national banks, trust companies and insurance firms, and when his own State Savings Bank of Butte, Montana, failed (along with United Copper itself) in October 1907, his other interests followed suit. News of the disaster, depositors' skittishness and the lack of any federal deposit insurance at the time seriously undermined public confidence, causing a panic, also known as a "run," on banks so severe that it had national and international ramifications. Some small-time operators even profited from the situation by holding places in lines of bank depositors outside failing institutions for a ten-dollar fee!

Under the leadership of the seventy-year-old J.P. Morgan, a group of bankers, financier's and government representatives met in the library of his palatial New York home and hammered out a deal whereby the banks and the U.S. Treasury would infuse the banking system with funds and help ease the crisis. The agreement even required then-president Theodore Roosevelt to sign an agreement that the government would not prosecute the group for antitrust violations that might arise from the deal. While the panic came to an end, essentially, by November 1, 1907, the economy was left in shambles, unemployment rose by 5 percent, the stock market crashed, production fell sharply and even the flow of immigrants from Europe slowed accordingly. The development of the Federal Reserve Bank and Federal Deposit Insurance Corporation were direct results of the panic.

Pardridge & Blackwell seemed flush and confident in its glamorous white palace of a home and was truly the "Heart of Detroit" as the illuminated, heart-shaped sign on its roof announced to the world. The Detroit papers were silent, but in the store's offices and in bank board rooms, the effect of the panic on the store's balance sheets was causing anxiety. The February 5, 1908 issue of *Men's Wear: The Retailer's Magazine* reported on the situation in Detroit, and in fact, an illustration entitled "Panic of Fall 1907" adorned the front cover and showed a caricature of a businessman labeled "Honesty and Integrity" running a path paved with the words "Money" and "Work" and lined by morning coat-wearing men wielding clubs labeled "Fake Advertising," "Graft," "Croesus," "Old Fixtures," "Pessimism" and "Get-Rich-Quick," among other ills of the day. The caption to this illustration read:

> *HE WILL WIN. He believes in himself. He knows what he wants. He will get it. YOU will have the same gauntlet to run. Do not heed those who stand at the side—with a club—the pessimists, grafters, fakirs [sic], liars, idlers or indifferent merchants.*

In the article itself, it was announced that Pardridge & Blackwell offered investors and note-holders stock in the company in return for an extension in payment terms (widely referred to at the time as an "embarrassment') and that its liabilities exceeded $1.1 million. This amount included unpaid invoices to merchandise vendors and amounts owed to depositors in the store's in-house bank. In fact, during the crisis, the bank had suffered a run just as others had, and it seriously compromised the store's balance sheet, as had some bad investments by the store in "inventions," such as the Safety Folding Bed Company, a precursor to the folding Murphy bed, which "did not take," according to the article, and "occasioned a fair-sized financial loss."

The article ends with mention that a member of a "prominent Toledo retail establishment" was involved in a plan to end the woes of Pardridge & Blackwell by investing $200,000 in the business and securing new loans of up to $100,000 to ensure further solvency and pay off creditors. The shopping public was apparently oblivious to the store's financial condition during and after the panic, as the *Detroit Free Press* reported on October 8 on the Pardridge & Blackwell's fall opening gala, saying:

> *"The Heart of Detroit"—Pardridge & Blackwell's institution—the most remarkable store in Detroit—different from all other stores in many ways, is celebrating its first autumn opening this week. Every window—twenty in all—artistically decorated with autumn foliage, and emblematic hearts of the same, is an eloquent demonstration of the highest artistic design*

in union of color and material. The superb effects are equal to any to be seen. A glance around the spacious quarters and the immensity of the stock, and the exclusiveness of the display, with the profusion of the decorations around the many pillars, and the large designs suspended from the ceilings, satisfies the onlooker that it is a piece of delight, whether he or she buys or not; but to the one in quest of unusual things it presents temptations quite beyond the powers of resistance.

Similarly, the store continued business as usual through the Christmas holiday season, the highlight of which was an after-hours gathering on the store's first floor at which employees presented Willard E. Pardridge and Henry Blackwell with a pair of lavishly executed loving cups as a gift of appreciation. A pall was cast over the store's operations in May when it became known that Marianne Josephine Blackwell, Henry Blackwell's wife, had become seriously ill.

Marianne Blackwell, hailed by the *Free Press* as a "noble woman," devoted herself to the charities of the Catholic Church in Detroit and supported the House of Providence, an institution run by the Daughters of Charity of St. Vincent DePaul for the benefit of unwed mothers and orphaned children. Willard Pardridge and Henry Blackwell donated six acres of property on Michigan Avenue near Dearborn (Pardridge & Walsh had earlier donated the property for the House of Providence's building on Grand Boulevard at Fourteenth Street) for use as a summer camp in 1903, no doubt at Mrs. Blackwell's instigation. The House of Providence eventually became Detroit's Providence Hospital.

Irish-born Marianne Blackwell passed away at the Blackwell home on May 18, 1908, at the age of fifty-two and was mourned across the city. Interestingly, the newspapers mentioned that this lady, who was "loved by the poor," had left Ireland on account of her involvement with the Home Rule movement in that country after the arrest of her uncle Father Quaid of O'Callahan's Mills, along with some of his supporters, of whom she was one. It wasn't until her death that Henry Blackwell's real reason for immigrating to the United States in 1890 was revealed. The couple was married in the parish church of Feenagh, County Limerick, in April 1888.

It was not until a year later that a bombshell was dropped on the city regarding "the most remarkable store in Detroit." A full-page ad in the Detroit newspapers on May 13, 1909, entitled "A New Name for an Old Firm" and announcing "Crowley, Milner & Co. succeed Pardridge & Blackwell" explained that Joseph J. Crowley of Detroit and William L.

A New Name For an Old Firm.

On July 13th last J. J. Crowley and W. L. Milner bought a controlling interest in this business. It was incorporated and W. L. Milner was made president and J. J. Crowley vice-president and treasurer.

The circumstances under which we were invited to identify ourselves with this prominent retail enterprise, need not here be discussed except to say that they were due to the disastrously strenuous times of 1908.

As is usual when new men with different ideas and methods come into control, many changes were soon determined on; all looking to greater economies in the operation of the business, to greater efficiency in the store organization, to better arrangement of the stocks and to better surroundings for our help.

Each and every such change or betterment has been most thoughtfully considered always with the best interests of the business at heart, and indirectly our customers' best interests as well. Gradually, and with as little friction as possible these changes have been introduced.

The first was the complete reorganization of our office and accounting systems with an entire change of process and the introduction of complete new systems of reports, etc.

The delivery system has also been entirely reorganized along lines which, when in thorough operation, will give this store the most efficient delivery system in the city.

Complete new store rules have been introduced, looking to greater efficiency in store service in all its details.

One change on which customers compliment us daily, and one entirely new in Detroit, although in successful operation in all the larger cities of the country is the establishment of an exchange desk, to which customers can take goods returned for exchange and be certain of prompt, pleasant, courteous treatment.

Many very important changes in the interior arrangements of the store were decided on and are now in process of execution. The offices and vaults have been removed from the balcony to the fifth floor, and now occupy commodious, well-lighted quarters, where the ventilation is of the best.

Crowley, Milner & Co.
SUCCEED
Pardridge & Blackwell

The old offices entirely lighted by electricity, and at the ceiling hight where the air was least desirable, especially in summer time, and with practically no ventilation at all, were, to say the least, very undesirable.

The Store Bank was closed at once, and the four thousand depositors paid their balances as fast as demanded.

This left the two ends of the balcony unoccupied, and realizing the great improvement in the store which would follow, we proceeded to remove them. This work is nearly completed, and we are complimented hourly on the great improvement in our store appearance.

Another change which has brought us marked commendation is the removal of the escalator, which obstructed the main aisle and occupied the most valuable space in the store. The novelty of such a means of passenger elevation having worn off, there seemed no good reason for continuing it. It has been removed.

Having great need for basement room in which to develop a *complete* housefurnishings and china department, and feeling that the grocery, meat and liquor departments were not a necessary adjunct to a dry goods store, we determined to discontinue them, and those of you who have benefitted by the sharp price reductions made during the closing out sale just completed, understand full well with what promptness and vigor we set about it. We have also discontinued the barber shop. We do not think it has any place in a store such as this is.

Several things planned for, and now being developed, will be of especial interest to every one at all interested in the welfare of store employes, and especially the women and girls of our store force.

One of these is: A locker room where each employe is provided with a ventilated steel locker for the inclosure under lock and key of their wraps during store hours.

Another is: A commodious rest room, amply provided with tables, magazines, rocking chairs, couches and divans, located on the sixth floor of the building, at the corner of the store where light and ventilation are best.

Any woman can readily understand how vitally important to the health and comfort of our female employes such a rest room is at lunch time, or any other time, when indisposed.

Ample sanitary and well-lighted and ventilated toilet rooms will also be installed for the use exclusively of our girls. These rooms will be under the constant care of a competent nurse and maid, who will look after the cleanliness of the rooms and the comfort of their users.

For the especial comfort of our lady customers we are now having plans drawn for a commodious and highly sanitary toilet and rest room on the third floor, which will have in conjunction, a sick room for the use and care of any woman who may be taken suddenly ill while in the store. These rooms will be equipped in the most approved and up-to-date manner, and we are certain will fill a long-felt want and remove the oft-expressed criticism of the failure of Detroit stores to provide such conveniences.

The one improvement which we are certain will jump into instant popularity will be a first-class restaurant, or tea room, for which the plans are now being completed and estimates being received. In this new restaurant the equipment will equal that of the very best store lunching rooms in any of the larger cities, and as the management will be in the hands of a highly capable department store caterer, the service will be of very high standard, while, following the well-known policy of this store, the prices will be most reasonable. The details of decoration we will leave for you to speculate on, and to enjoy when completed.

Other changes are also being considered, many of vital importance to some part or other of this business, to which your attention will be called from time to time.

And now the greatest change of all, a change in the firm name.

This business will hereafter be the Crowley, Milner & Co. business. At the solicitation of Messrs. Willard E. Pardridge and Henry Blackwell, we have bought from them at a very substantial figure all their remaining interest in the business, and they will now retire from all connection with it.

The conclusion to change the firm name was reached with full appreciation of the great value of the good will attached to it. We do so, however, in order that we may sail under no false colors, in order that you may know in truth and at once who is responsible for this business and its policies.

That the business will be run with courage and aggressively up to our highest conviction of the things we think are best for it, we assure you.

That the vital part of storekeeping, the real buying and selling of goods, shall meet your approval, that the completeness and selection of our stocks shall win your favor, that the store service shall be such as to leave no room for complaint, be assured, as is our determination to build up here in this city, and in this building, the strongest store organization which can be brought together, a store force such as will sweep this business at once into pronounced leadership.

There will be no change in the store's policy. This store always has been, and shall still be, the store of all stores best suited for the great majority of the people to trade in. We will tolerate no misstatements or misrepresentations, either at our counter or in our advertising. Every dollar's worth of goods we sell will take with it our definite guarantee that it will give you proper satisfaction, a full measure of money's worth.

Equal attention and consideration will be given all alike, be they rich or poor; old or young; elegantly or plainly clad. It will be as heretofore, a democratic store, not only as regards its attitude to its customers, but also as regards the relationships between the store force, as it is our position that there are no social inequalities in the store force, and no more exercise of authority than is necessary to the perfection of good store service and the efficient building up of the business.

It is our earnest desire to so run this business as to please you best; to make this in truth the one great family store of Michigan; to build up here, in this beautiful city, such a retail enterprise as shall command the enthusiastic pride of every Detroit citizen.

Look to us then, for the best that in us lies. Condone our mistakes. Help us with your suggestions. Take a personal interest in our progress and development. Come to know this as one of Detroit's most substantial, dependable establishments.

Crowley, Milner & Co.
Successors to Pardridge & Blackwell

Even though they took over operation of Pardridge & Blackwell in July 1908, the new owners didn't announce their new name and improved business practices until March 1909 with this article. *Collection of the author.*

Milner of Toledo had purchased a controlling interest in the business due to "the disastrously strenuous times of 1908." Elsewhere, the ad mentioned that Crowley and Milner had now bought out Pardridge's & Blackwell's remaining interests and that the former owners would now "retire from all connection with it." Furthermore, the closure of the basement grocery department and mezzanine banking office were accomplished because the new owners felt strongly that such operations didn't belong in a proper department store.

Surprisingly, the new owners didn't think much of escalators, either, and it might surprise many who rode the beautiful wooden escalators in Crowley's up until the 1970s that they were not original to the building. The ad announcing the new Crowley, Milner & Co., after admonishing that "when new men with different ideas and methods come into control, many changes were determined on," stated:

> *Another change which has brought us marked commendation is the removal of the esculator* [sic] *which obstructed the main aisle and occupied the most valuable space in the store. The novelty of such a means of passenger elevation having worn off, there seemed no good reason for continuing it. It has been removed.*

Another reason the so-called esculator may have failed to gain longevity is that early models of the now-ubiquitous device lacked the entrance and exit landings of more modern models, and from photographs and descriptions of them, an ascent on one could be a fairly harrowing experience.

New facilities and improvements for customers and employees had already been put in place, such as new offices on the fifth floor surrounded by windows and provided with natural light and ventilation, a central exchange desk on the first floor to satisfy the company's policy of prompt and friendly returns and exchanges of merchandise that didn't prove satisfactory and an improved and expanded delivery service for customers who chose not to carry purchases home on Detroit's vast street railways network.

In the future, Crowley, Milner & Co. planned to provide an expanded china, gift and glassware selection on the basement level, better facilities for the welfare of workers and a proper tearoom to serve lunch and refreshments to customers. The full-page ad stated that the restaurant "will equal that of the very best store lunching rooms in any of the larger cities." It concluded its description of the coming tearoom by saying, "The details of decoration we will leave for you to speculate on, and to enjoy when completed."

The ad ended by saying:

> *It is our earnest desire to run this business as to please you best; to make this in truth the one great family store of Michigan; to build up here, in*

Until Crowley's began expanding over the block, it looked like Pardridge & Blackwell, albeit with a massive new sign. Inside, things changed in keeping with the new store management's dynamic vision. *Courtesy of Michael Hauser.*

> *this beautiful city, such a retail enterprise as shall command the enthusiastic pride of every Detroit citizen. Look to us then, for the best that in us lies. Condone our mistakes. Help us with your suggestions. Take a personal interest in our progress and development. Come to know this as one of Detroit's most substantial, dependable establishments.*

Of course, in 1908 Detroit, Joseph J. Crowley was well enough known on account of his involvement with the Crowley Brothers wholesale business, which, by 1908, had grown into one of the largest in the region. Even after Crowley and Milner bought their interest in Pardridge & Blackwell's store, the wholesale firm that involved Joseph Crowley's brothers Daniel as vice-president and William as secretary continued to expand along Jefferson Avenue into a major presence. William Milner of Toledo, as a customer of Crowley Brothers, was known to the brothers, but his name was not familiar in Detroit. On the day that the Crowley, Milner & Co. name was introduced to the public, the *Detroit Free Press* informed them that Milner

> *has for many years conducted the largest and most successful department store in Toledo. He is recognized as Toledo's leading business representative and is president of Chamber of Commerce of that city. In business circles in the city on the Maumee, Mr. Milner is recognized everywhere as one of the brightest, most successful and progressive department store men in the country.*

The growth, stability and magnitude of Milner's Toledo store certainly confirmed the paper's description, as did an article in the February 6, 1904 issue of the *Dry Goods Reporter*. Boasting that "Few towns and cities can claim so beautiful a store as the Milner store," the article went on to tell the story in plain facts: Toledo's biggest store had over five hundred employees, 200,000 square feet of floor space, 300 lineal feet of show windows, three entrances, four elevators and two main aisles 180 feet in length—and that was just a precursory list. Milner's big store, situated on Toledo's bustling Front Street and anchoring the south end of the shopping district, was the result of the meteoric rise of its founder.

Hailing from Atlanta, Illinois, Milner eventually moved to Hartford, Kansas, where he successfully developed a local dry goods store into a $60,000-per-year operation, quite a remarkable accomplishment in a town of not more than eight hundred inhabitants. Interestingly, when Milner decided, like many successful merchants, that a move to a bigger city would broaden his opportunities, he engaged in discussions with his primary wholesaler, the Burnham-Hanna-Munger Dry Goods Company of Kansas City, which was the affiliate of Burnham, Stoepel & Company of Detroit, where Joseph J. Crowley had worked prior to the formation of Crowley Brothers.

From Mr. Munger of the Kansas City wholesaler, Milner learned of a retail house, the R.L. McElroy store in Toledo, Ohio, that was ripe for purchase. Milner bought the store in 1895 and eventually put his own name on it. Given his retail expertise, the store was able to double sales within a year, confounding naysayers who predicted failure on account of the store's location and size, which was deemed too large for the market. However, according the *Toledo Blade*, "The people of the city liked the nerve and novelty of the thing, and from the day the doors opened, the store became one of the show-spots of Toledo." Milner attributed his success to "hard work and doing things right. Most people have good ideas and their plans are all right, but they never execute them."

An expansion of Milner's great Toledo store was announced in May 1903 and built in stages until a formal grand opening of the store with "excellent music" and "attractive souvenirs" was held on December 11, 1906. Clearly, a number of features of Milner's store certainly presaged the transition of Detroit's old Pardridge & Blackwell into the "new Crowley, Milner & Co." in a few years to come. Milner's was known for its beautiful restaurant, the fact that it sold no groceries and the prolific advertising carried on by the store under Milner's direction. Milner was convinced that a successful department store's promotions were key to drawing customers, and as a result, the store had an auditorium, which he called a "theaterette," installed on the store's fifth floor adjacent to the restaurant, which overlooked the Maumee River and was said to be "perfectly equipped."

In fact, Milner's store was a customer of the Crowley brothers' wholesale business, and when Detroit's Central Savings Bank (which had moved into the ground floor of the Majestic Building after Pardridge & Blackwell vacated it) offered the Crowleys attractive loan rates to take over the failing

William Milner's operation on Front Street in downtown Toledo, Ohio, grew to become the largest department store between Cleveland and Chicago under his guidance. *From a postcard, collection of the author.*

business, bringing Milner into the deal was natural because of his exemplary retail experience. Accordingly, Milner became the president of the new store and Joseph J. Crowley the vice-president. It all happened fairly smoothly and without much publicity until Crowley, Milner & Co. made its announcement in 1909.

Though removed from the store that once bore their name, Willard Pardridge and Henry Blackwell were back in the news by June 1909. Pardridge purchased the dry goods business known as Sparling's, located at 155–57 Woodward Avenue. After a closeout of the store's old stock, it was announced that the new business, to be named Henry Blackwell & Co., would open on the site. The grand opening was held on September 2, 1909, and Detroit's ever-changing and volatile retail marketplace took yet another turn. Their store was not mentioned in the press after 1916, and it can safely be assumed that it was not the success that the partners had hoped. Crowley, Milner & Co. had, however, arrived and would become a foundation of Detroit's shopping scene for years to come.

6

FAMILY PLOT

*G*iven the way that Crowley and Milner assumed control over the former Pardridge & Blackwell store—first purchasing a controlling interest, then operating it for a time to get a feel for its pulse and its customers and making a big announcement about a name change only after they had tested some of their methods and acquired complete control—Detroit shoppers assumed they were there to stay. The point was made even more strongly as the promised improvements and changes in the store's operation were put into service and the business took hold and became a Detroit institution in its own right. Meanwhile, Crowley's home, Detroit, acquired fame as a growing city, where new jobs were being created and wealth was being built, especially as a result of the expansion of the auto industry. Detroit's boulevards and fine buildings gave it a reputation as the "Paris of North America," and the lofty moniker was not exactly undeserved.

Crowley's literally rode Detroit's wave. In November 1909, the store opened its fourth-floor restaurant and revamped the basement one already in operation. When its second-floor hairdressing salon opened in early 1910, the *Detroit Free Press* proclaimed it "the finest in Detroit." With success came pressure on the existing physical plant, and Crowley's began an expansion program that would eventually see the store consume the whole block bounded by Gratiot Avenue, Farmer Street, Monroe Avenue, Library Street (then known as Farrar Street) and then some.

Some idea of Crowley's early success can be seen in the fact that, less than a year after the new Crowley, Milner & Co. signs went up on the

Luncheon

SERVED 11 A. M. TO 2:30 P. M

SEA FOOD, ETC.

Blue Points on Half Shell 25   Oysters, Provençale 35   Baked Oysters 30
Oyster Stew (milk) 25   Oyster Stew (cream) 35
Scolloped Oysters 30   Fried Oysters (½ doz.) 25
Lobster or Crab Meat Cocktail 25   Little Neck Clams (½ Dozen) 25
Broiled Live Lobster (½) 50; whole 90 Lobster or Crabmeat, à la Newburg 50
Cold Boiled Lobster, Mayonnaise 50-90   Whitefish, Broiled 35; Planked 45
Fried Pickerel, Tartar Sauce 30   Fried Lake Perch 30   Baked Lake Trout 30

RELISHES

Sliced Tomatoes 20   Sliced Cucumbers 15   Celery Hearts 15
New Radishes 10   Young Onions 10
Sweet Mixed Pickles 10   Ripe Olives 10   Stuffed Olives 10   Dill Pickles 10
Pickled Walnuts 15   Salted Almonds 15

SOUPS

Homemade Bean Soup 15   Chicken Broth with Noodles 15

Consommé in Cup 15   Hot Clam Bouillon 15

TODAY'S SPECIALS-READY TO SERVE

Broiled Whitefish 30   Lamb Fries, Breaded, Tomato Sauce 30
Fried Scollops with Bacon 35
Pork and Marrowfat Beans 15
Minced Chicken on Toast 35
Roast Leg of Veal with Dressing 20
Roast Prime Beef, Natural Gravy 25 ; Extra Cut 40

SPECIALS TO ORDER (10 TO 15 MINUTES)

Finnan Haddie (Chafing Dish) 50   Sweetbread or Oyster Patties 35
Chicken, à la King 75 (Chafing Dish)   Welsh Rarebit 30
Calf's Sweetbread, Newburg 50 (Chafing Dish)   Chicken Croquettes 35
Imported Frankfurts, Potato Salad 30   Philadelphia Squab on Toast 50
Broiled or Fried Spring Chicken on Toast, half 50; whole 90
Fried Frog Legs, half doz. 35   Calf's Sweetbread, Sauté, Mushrooms 40

STEAKS, CHOPS, CUTLETS (15 MINUTES)

Sirloin Steak 75   Little Pig Sausage 30   Extra Porterhouse Steak 1.25
Small Steak 50   Pork Chops 25   Tenderloin Steak 50
Breaded Veal Cutlets 25; Tomato Sauce 30   Lamb Chops 35   Broiled Ham 25
Fried Ham 25   Ham and Eggs 35   Bacon and Eggs 35   Broiled Bacon 25

VEGETABLES

Green Peas 10   Brussels Sprouts 15   Spiced Beets 10
Spinach 10   Mashed Squash 10
Potatoes in Cream 10   French Fried Potatoes 15
Hashed Browned Potatoes 15 Saratoga Chips 10 Potatoes, au Gratin 15
Mashed, Boiled Potatoes 5 Browned Potatoes 5 Browned Sweet Potatoes 10

EGGS AND OMELETS

Plain Omelet 25   Ham Omelet 30   Poached Eggs on Toast 20
Scrambled Eggs 20   Fried Eggs 15
Boiled Eggs (two) 15   Shirred Eggs 15

DAIRY LUNCHEONS

Corn Muffins 5   Rolls 5   Graham Bread 5
Boston Brown Bread 5   Dry or Buttered Toast 10   Cream Toast 20
Milk Toast 15   Wheat Flakes 15   Corn Flakes 15
Shredded Wheat Biscuit 15   Flaked Rice 15
Zwieback 10   Bread or Crackers and Milk 15   Toasted English Muffins 15

BREAD AND BUTTER SERVED WITH ALL MEAT AND FISH ORDERS
KINDLY REPORT ANY INATTENTION TO THE MANAGEMENT

AFTERNOON TEA SERVED FROM 2:30 TO 5:30 P. M.

DETROIT'S FRIENDLY STORE

November 21, 1910

COLD MEATS

TELEPHONE AT CASHIER'S DESK

Cold Roast Beef, Potato Salad 30   Cold Roast Turkey 35
Cold Boiled Ham, Potato Salad 30   Kalter Aufschnitte 40
Cold Boiled Fresh Beef Tongue with Potato Salad 30
Cold Roast Chicken, Potato Salad 35   **Imported Westphalia Ham 40**

SALADS

Lettuce and Tomato 25   Green Pepper 20
Cold Slaw 15   Pineapple 25   Lettuce 20   Head Lettuce 25
Chicken 30   Combination 25   Romaine 25   Lobster 35   Potato 15
Tomato 25   Shrimp 35   Spiced Beets 10   Salmon 30
Macédoine 35   Celery 20   Fruit 25   **Sliced Tomatoes 20**

SANDWICHES

Club Sandwich 35   Sardine Sandwich 20   Fried Egg Sandwich 15
Chicken Sandwich 20   Lettuce Sandwich 10
Minced or Sliced Ham Sandwich 15   Imported Swiss Cheese Sandwich 15
Tongue Sandwich 15   Hot Roast Beef Sandwich 25
Ham and Egg Sandwich 25

PASTRY AND DESSERT

Rice Pudding 10
Sliced Apple Pie 10   Pear Pie 10   **Custard Pie 10**
Fruit Jelly 10   Cream Puffs 10   **Cup Custard 10**
French Pastry 10   Swiss Cream Meringue 15   **German Coffee Cake 10**
Charlotte Russe 10   Chocolate Eclairs 10

CAKES, ICES AND CREAMS

(WE MAKE OUR OWN ICE CREAM)
Layer Cake 10   White Cake 10   Chocolate Cake 10
Macaroons 10   Chocolate Ice Cream 10   Meringue Glacé 20   Angel Cake 10
Mixed Ices and Creams 15
Orange Sherbet 10   Coupe, St. Jacques 25   Pineapple Sherbet 10
Ice Cream: Vanilla or Neapolitan 10, Cafe Parfait 15; Alaska 50

FRUITS

Sliced Oranges 10   Sliced Bananas with Cream 10   Stewed Prunes 10
Bar-le-Duc 20   Orange Marmalade 10   Sliced Pineapple 10
Currant Jelly 15   **Grapes 15**   Homemade Quince Jelly 15   Figs in Syrup 10
Baked Apple with Cream 10   Grapefruit 15; with Maraschino 25

CHEESE

American 10   Imported Swiss 15   Roquefort 15
Camembert 15   Pimiento 15   Gorgonzola 15   Neufchatel 10

BEVERAGES

Cup of Hot Water with Cream 5   Pot Coffee, one order 5
Pot Coffee, two orders 10   Pot Chocolate 10
Pot Lipton's No. 1 Ceylon Tea 5
Pot English Breakfast Tea 5   Pot Japan Tea 5
Malted Milk, Hot or Iced 15

ICED BEVERAGES

Walker-Gordon Buttermilk 10   Iced Tea 5   **Lactase 5**   Grape Juice 5
Glass of Milk 5   Glass of Cream 15
Iced Coffee 10   **Lemonade, (to order) 10**
Glass Half Cream and Half Milk 10   **Sweet Cider 5**
Apollinaris Lemonade 20   Apollinaris Water, half Pint 15
Apollinaris Water, Pint 25   White Rock Water, half Pint 15

Not Responsible for Wearing Apparel Left in Dining Room

SPECIAL DINNER SERVED FROM 5:30 TO 8:00 P. M. ON SATURDAYS.

ALL PRICES BASED ON SERVICE FOR ONE

Above and opposite: In 1909, Crowley's opened an elegant tearoom that "took up practically the whole fourth floor," according to reports of the day. Frog legs, an unusual item for a department store eatery, became a specialty remembered to this day. *Courtesy of Michael Hauser.*

79

building, the store advertised that it had acquired an adjacent structure, just vacated by furniture store Owen & Company, which moved from its Gratiot Avenue address into a new Albert Kahn–designed building on Grand River Avenue. After the purchase, Crowley's began a liquidation sale in its third-floor men's departments so it could open a new men's store in the former Owen building. Crowley's boasted:

> *The immense increase in trade now coming to Crowley-Milner's has been the talk of all who come in contact with the store, and is positive assurance that the public know and appreciate the things that have already been accomplished in providing better service, more comforts and conveniences and greater benefits in the way of good merchandising for the patrons of the store. Yet, of all these things, as remarkable as they seem, are but the beginning of the important steps that will soon be made. The store is just getting its stride. The securing of the Owen Building clears the way for the immediate changes and improvements that are to follow, and we are now free to carry out the larger plans that we have been carefully studying out for several months back. These improvements involve the re-arrangement of practically every floor in the entire store, giving us the opportunity to arrange each department JUST AS WE WANT IT. This will relieve the congestion of the main floor and provide the necessary space, everywhere, to obtain the utmost comfort in shopping.*

It would seem that Crowley's would take these words as a guiding principle for years to come and that the "larger plans" referred to would later reveal themselves as the store acquired the whole city block on which it stood. Just a little over two months after the new men's store announcement, Crowley's made public that it had signed a fifteen-year lease on the building next to the Owen store, known as the Latham, Weber & Co. Building, which extended all the way to Library Street. In the fall of 1910, the store's gala autumn fashion opening was advertised as "Crowley-Milner's in Full Panoply" and included an illustration of the store with both newly acquired properties. By then, Crowley's had even bought the small, thirty-three-foot-wide building that housed Pardridge & Blackwell's men's furnishings shop on Monroe Avenue, which was connected to the first floor of the main store by means of an archway.

On November 20, 1910, the press reported that a smaller competitor, Goldberg Brothers, had plans to build an eight-story department store block on Gratiot Avenue, across Library Street from Crowley's newly acquired properties.

When the building, clad in white terra cotta like the nearby Crowley edifice, opened in May 1912, the *Detroit Free Press* called the new home of the twenty-five-year-old Goldberg Brothers store a "veritable shoppers' paradise" and marveled at the design by local architect Richard H. Marr, which allowed light to stream in from all sides of the building. Eventually, two more floors were added to it.

In spite of the proximity of the Goldberg Brothers store, not to mention the growing Hudson establishment on the other side of the Detroit Public Library, Crowley's went from strength to strength, and a few days after the New Year celebrations of 1916, it informed the public that it had acquired or leased all remaining properties on the block and planned to commence construction of an eight-story building that would in all aspects, save for its seventh- and eighth-floor colonnades, match the original six-story Pardridge & Blackwell structure. Two years after the new addition was completed, it was announced that two more floors would be added to the 1907 building, creating a cohesive whole covering the block and distinguished by its gleaming white façades. Alas, the original building's beautiful and elaborate cornice had to be removed to accommodate the new floors, which were completed in 1921.

In 1917, Crowley, Milner & Co. purchased the Goldberg Brothers store across Library Street and changed its name to "The Emporium," which it operated as a subsidiary. The Emporium only lasted about three years, and the construction of a tunnel connecting its building to Crowley's main store was a sign that something was up. On April 16, 1920, the Emporium let the public know that it was being closed and that Crowley's earlier purchase of the business anticipated temporary operation of it as an independent store only until the parent store needed the space. Crowley's then went about relocating departments in the Goldberg building and completing the tunnel connecting the two buildings. In September 1920, Crowley's new Store for Homes was opened to appropriate fanfare.

The *Grand Rapids Furniture Review* of January 1921 gave an account of the new, 100,000-square-foot store, saying that the Store for Homes

> *is a radical step in furniture merchandising by department stores, this being the first exclusive store of the kind to be started by a department store. It should prove an inspiration to furniture merchants and force them to the realization that unless they awake to a full cognizance of their opportunities, the department stores will pass them or replace them. The Crowley, Milner & Co. store was opened late last year opposite*

the big department store and already this company's business in home furnishings has shown a healthy growth…it is now one of the city's finest merchandising establishments, rearing its head over most of the buildings surrounding the park which it faces.

The journal went on to describe the building's layout floor by floor, from the china and kitchenware departments in the basement; the drapery department ("a welcome sight to shoppers because of its beauty") on the first floor; and electrical appliances, lamps and records on the second. It made mention of the two floors of rugs (the third and fourth) as well as the expansive linoleum display on the fifth floor, noting that Crowley's "had the reputation of doing the largest linoleum business" of any store in the country. A picture gallery and wallpaper selections could be found on the sixth floor, and the store's furniture galleries occupied the next three floors above that. On the tenth, top-most floor could be found bedding and mattresses.

One important feature of the Store for Homes was a branch office of the Industrial Morris Plan Bank on the seventh floor. Ever since Crowley's closed Pardridge & Blackwell's in-house bank in 1908, the new store operated on a cash basis. The Morris Plan, however, offered customers an opportunity to finance large purchases at attractive rates. The plan was developed by Arthur J. Morris in Norfolk, Virginia, as a method of offering attractive term-payment purchases to working-class Americans. Eventually, the plan spread to one hundred locations across the country, and in spite of its rejection of Pardridge & Blackwell's banking scheme, Crowley's management welcomed the Industrial Morris Plan Bank with open arms as a customer service and a method of increasing sales through credit options in the era before department store credit cards.

If the rapid growth of Crowley's in the early years was fueled by the expansion of the automobile industry (Henry Ford and Ford vice-president James Couzens announced that they were doubling workers' wages to five dollars per day in January 1914), the flames of the store's expansion were fanned by the partnership of the Crowleys and William Milner, who brought their wealth of experience and talent to bear on the young retail operation. All of that was to change on the evening of August 17, 1922.

Milner, who had been working in Detroit at Crowley's, was returning southbound to Toledo on the Dixie Highway when he decided to pass a truck loaded with automobile frames on the two-lane road. When he swerved to the left to avoid an oncoming car he had not noticed, his new Stutz vehicle slipped off the road onto the gravel shoulder, went out of control and rolled into a ditch. Milner was pinned under the car, crushing his chest, and only the steering wheel, which bore the full weight of the car, saved Milner from being killed on the spot. Incredibly, though the *Toledo News-Bee* reports mentioned the high speeds at which the crash occurred, eyewitnesses confirmed that Milner's car was traveling "at about 30 miles per hour." Joseph J. Crowley's wife later revealed that Milner had long tried to make each of his successive biweekly trips home in less time than the one before, in spite of his friends' and colleagues' forebodings regarding the practice.

Photos of the grisly scene adorned the front page of the *Toledo News-Bee*, and reporters described a picture of scattered suitcases and golf clubs and described Milner as he was pulled out of the wreck, noting that "his face was black from shock and the rush of blood." Reports from the hospital on subsequent days were hopeful because complications from Milner's injuries did not set in immediately. However, on the morning of Saturday, September 2, he was diagnosed with a pulmonary embolism as a result of his injuries and died shortly afterward. His wife and daughter were at his side, and he was laid to rest a few days later.

Toledo didn't just lose a top-class merchant, it also lost a man of character who had a true sense of civic duty. He served on the Toledo Chamber of Commerce and headed the committee that organized Toledo's streetcar service. The plan he promoted, which was later implemented, was referred to as the "Milner Plan" on account of his influence over it. He also served on the boards of many Toledo-based banks and corporations. Milner was predeceased by his son John, who died when he fell four floors down an open elevator shaft in his father's store.

Detroit, too, felt the loss of Crowley, Milner & Co.'s president. Crowley's remained closed on September 5, 1922, the day of Milner's funeral and tributes came in from the businesses and organizations with which he was associated. The biggest effect on Crowley's was, of course, that it had lost its president but also an owner of over one-half of the store's stock. Milner's store in Toledo foundered under the management of his heirs in the years after his death, and even renaming it the "New Milner's" couldn't stave off its demise in 1928. Crowley's faced a similar fate, but the continuity provided by the Crowley family, and the appointment of Joseph J. Crowley to the post of president vacated by Milner, helped the store continue its growth and market penetration. In fact, Willard P. Emery, general manager of Crowley, Milner & Co., was soon able to purchase the interest of Milner's wife and daughter in the Detroit business and may have spared it the fate of the older store in Toledo.

Another blow came on November 1, 1925, when Joseph J. Crowley died of a heart attack in his home at 243 Lakeland Avenue in Grosse Pointe. Even more so than in Milner's case, tributes poured in and his accomplishments were recalled on the occasion of his death at age sixty-three. Joseph Crowley's life as a merchant, a trade he learned in his father's Corktown grocery store, was only equaled by his service to the organizations of his city and the Roman Catholic Church. Outside of directing his considerable business ventures, he served five years on the Board of Water Commissioners in the administration of Mayor William Maybury, later served on the Detroit Board of Commerce and was a founding member of the Knights of Columbus in the city. In addition, he was a member of the boards of three of Detroit's leading banks.

The listing of his accomplishments was only eclipsed by the personal tributes that were printed in the press following his demise. Well-known former mayor John C. Lodge recalled that he played amateur baseball with his friend "Joe" and called him "a man of great brain and heart and a genius for friendship." Current mayor John W. Smith recalled:

> *Joseph Crowley was one of Detroit's most useful citizens. He was identified with every movement for the welfare of the city and I, with thousands of fellow citizens, admired his integrity, his broad-mindedness and his unqualified devotion to every cause. I know that the people of Detroit, of every class and creed, will sincerely regret his passing.*

Fellow retailer Edward J. Hickey, founder of the men's store E.J. Hickey Company, added:

> *To us who knew him, the memory of Joseph Crowley recalls his genius as a builder, his rare judgement and his courage. Many successful merchants of the city of the city and state owe their success to his wise counsel. Those who were born in Detroit and were privileged with his friendship from boyhood knew Mr. Crowley for his loyalty and devotion to the finer things of life—his country, his friends, and his faith—and for his open-hearted generosity to the poor and afflicted. I sincerely consider him a real Christian.*

Crowley was succeeded by his wife, Jenny (née Flynn), whom he had married in 1896. The demure Mrs. Crowley learned about her husband's business when he returned to their home after twelve-hour days at the store. The couple grew fond of talking until late in the evening over a cup of coffee, and Crowley often solicited his wife's "feminine intuition"

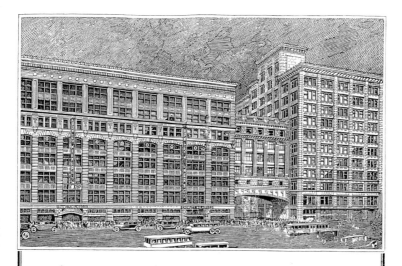

Better Prepared to Serve

The entire purpose of this great store is to serve the homes and families of Greater Detroit. To that end we strive to give values and render a service that will satisfy most of the wants of all the people all the time.

The new year finds us better prepared to serve the people of Detroit and environs than we have ever been before. This is a greatly improved store—with hundreds of new fixtures—a new main floor—wider aisles —more spacious departments—new entrances and further improvements in the making! Better elevator facilities—improved show windows that we may adequately display our merchandise—and other improvements to follow during the year that will once again demonstrate that this is truly a store of progress—keeping its physical surroundings in pace with its greatly enlarged and more complete stocks of better merchandise— with a confidence in the future and prosperity of Detroit that emphatically bears out our slogan—

"A Great Store in a Great City"

Crowley, Milner & Co.

By 1925, Crowley's had expanded its physical plant to practically 800,000 square feet and connected its Main Building and East Building with an iconic bridge. *Courtesy of Michael Hauser.*

about the marketability of products and the proper merchandise mix for the family store. Jenny Crowley took her husband's place on the board of directors in 1925 and held the post for over thirty-one years; she was a familiar presence on the Jefferson bus since she rode downtown two or three times weekly to check out goings-on at the store or to attend board meetings.

In spite of the loss of its founders, Crowley's continued to prosper and grow. In 1923, a new eleven-story addition to the "East Building," as the Store for Homes became known, fronting on Monroe Avenue, was begun. After approval from the city planning commission, a handsome arched bridge clad in white terra cotta connected floors three through seven of the two buildings and spanned Library Street. The store's 1925 New Year ad promised customers:

> Soon the rattling of the riveting hammer will resound again on Crowley, Milner property. For the fourth time in less than sixteen years the machine gun of progress will be pressed into service to enlarge the facilities of this live retail business. A new building of steel and concrete will be reared on the northeast corner of Monroe and Library Avenues. A five-story bridge will span Library Avenue to connect the two units of the bigger and better Crowley, Milner's. To all outward appearances this new building will be a duplicate of the present Store for Homes with which it will connect on every floor. Inwardly it will represent a higher development in efficient organization. A building is but a mass of steel and concrete—a shell—until the throbbing, vibrating pulse of activity is put within it. It is because the men and women who make up this organization have made expansion necessary that we are erecting this new unit. We frankly proclaim it a tribute to the energy and resourcefulness of the organization gathered together, trained and fostered by the founders of this business. This program of expansion bears mute evidence of an organization's faith in the future of this great city. Crowley, Milner's is one of the fastest growing stores in the United States. A stringent policy of short profits and quick turnover has made this Store one of the marvels of the mercantile world—A policy which receives further expansion in the building of this newest addition.

While the bridge was distinguished for its rich classical detailing—which included three-story fluted pilasters capped with stylized phoenixes, elaborate floral bosses between the seventh-floor windows and a balustrade at the parapet—its two large clocks made it an instant landmark. Another innovation introduced in 1925 was Crowley's Bargain Basement, a separate store offering off-price merchandise in the below-ground salesroom that once housed Pardridge & Blackwell's grocery store that was discontinued by Joseph Crowley and William Milner. When the Store for Homes opened in

The new East Building extension on Monroe Avenue towered ten floors above the street, but this view also shows the eleventh-floor penthouse. The familiar clock on the beautifully detailed bridge is visible as well. *From the Manning Brothers Historic Photograph Collection.*

1920, Crowley's china and glass selections were relocated across the street, making the basement redundant until the Bargain Basement was introduced in 1925.

Less than two years after Joseph Crowley's death, his brother William passed away at his flat in the Whittier Hotel on Jefferson Avenue on the

Detroit River. William Crowley was survived by his wife, Elizabeth, and his two daughters. He was remembered as one of the driving forces behind the Crowley Brothers wholesale business, which was ultimately dissolved in the early 1920s, and a fine athlete who played baseball on the winning team of the Detroit Athletic Club.

William Crowley's obituary made mention of an interesting fact. He was one of a few survivors of a terrible tragedy that took place on the Detroit River on July 23, 1880. The Reverend Father A.F. Bleyenburg of Holy Trinity Church had hired the steam yacht *Mamie* to take altar boys and parish staff on a pleasure cruise to Monroe, Michigan. Upon its return, at ten o'clock in the evening, the craft collided with the large excursion steamer *Garland*, which was loaded with 1,200 passengers. The bigger vessel sliced the *Mamie* in two, sinking it immediately and causing the death of 17 of the 25 lives on board. Of the 16 altar boys on the excursion, only 4, William Crowley among them, were pulled from the water. Even more interesting is

Crowley, Milner & Co. as seen from the corner of Gratiot Avenue and Farmer Street. This image shows the store after all of the improvements of the 1920s were completed. *Courtesy of Michael Hauser.*

the fact that the 4 survivors grew up to become businessmen who reached the pinnacle of their industries, as though the brush with death gave them the wherewithal to succeed.

The turbulent years that saw the death of William L. Milner and the two Crowley brothers came to a conclusion in late 1927, when the Crowley family was able to buy back control of the store by purchasing the shares of Willard P. Emery. At a November 9 meeting inside the halls of the Detroit Trust Company, control of Crowley, Milner & Co. reverted definitively to the Crowley family, and the company's management was reorganized. Daniel T. Crowley was named president, while Joseph and Jenny Crowley's son, Daniel J. Crowley, became vice-president. Jenny Crowley remained on the board, along with William Crowley's widow, Elizabeth, who joined the board as a trustee for her daughters, Elizabeth and Katherine. Jenny Crowley and her son, Daniel, carried the additional responsibility of being trustees for Joseph and Jenny's three daughters, Helen, Marjorie and Mrs. Katherine De Hull Travis.

The *Detroit Free Press* noted that the executive shuffle that put the Crowley family back in the driver's seat at Crowley, Milner & Co. marked "the beginning of a new era in the meteoric rise of this store." The Crowley family wasted no time modernizing and improving the business in spite of the Great Depression looming on the horizon.

7

THE FRIENDLY STORE

With Crowley, Milner & Co. now back in the firm control of the Crowley family, no time was wasted in improving the store's physical plant. And well it should have been upgraded, for this was the era of the J.L. Hudson Company's remarkable growth into one of the world's largest stores. In fact, at a colossal 2.3 million square feet of space, Hudson's dwarfed Crowley's arguably more beautiful but smaller store of 793,934 square feet. Furthermore, it was time to assert that Crowley's was now (mostly) family owned, and the people responsible for the extraordinary transformation of the store in the years after its founding wanted to give the public something to talk about.

The big changes were preceded by scaffolding and construction hoarding all around the store's main floor. In the center of the light, lofty floor, a big and somewhat startling change was underway as well. The store planned all of the improvements in conjunction with its nineteenth-anniversary celebration, and a major sale was planned for April. One by one, the barricades came down to reveal something new to shoppers who had been putting up with the inconvenience, noise and confusion for months. The first revelation came just before the nineteenth-anniversary sale. In spite of the fact that one of Joseph Crowley's and William Milner's first changes at Pardridge & Blackwell was to remove the old escalator, dismissing it as a novelty, new ones ("Ten flights of them!" according to an announcement) were installed right in the center of the Main Building. Beautifully clad in deeply toned and varnished walnut paneling, the new conveyances took pressure off a store whose elevators alone could not handle the ever-increasing customer traffic.

Ads heralding the sale and the fact that the escalators would be ready tempted customers with the news that "the big barricades that have been up in our main building for several months will be taken down this week" and that "no longer will you have to wait or walk—just step onto an escalator and be taken up or down with comfort and rapidity." In addition, Crowley's ads forecasted that the store would have "3,000 Extra Salespeople—Cashiers—Wrappers!" in place by Saturday, April 28, for the sale and to alleviate crowding it said was "our problem of handling the crowds that daily patronize Crowley-Milner's." Photographs of Detroit's downtown shopping area, and indeed the streets that bordered the brilliant white buildings of Crowley's, bear out the congestion that resulted from such healthy commerce in the center of Detroit.

It was planned that the first day of the sale would be called "Crowley-Milner Day," and ads were created to pique the public interest by revealing that "The Whole Town Is Talking" and that

> *every man, woman and child in Detroit knows that when this store promises something unusual—something unusual is going to happen…nineteen years of intensive merchandising are back of this event. Six months ago we began the preparations and plans which are culminating Saturday in the biggest day's selling this store has ever enjoyed.*

Indeed, something unusual happened. After three full-page ads packed with merchandise beckoned customers, a record number—275,000 people—packed the store on Crowley-Milner Day, and a one-day sales record was smashed. An old copy of *Crowley's Round Up* employee magazine reported that Henry Horngren, who worked in the store's kitchens, remembered that the six thousand employees working on that day were too busy to take lunch breaks, and Horngren's staff had to "work like beavers to deliver sandwiches, which salespeople gulped down as they wrote out sales checks."

The new wooden escalators worked their magic, assisted by a contest that raised customers' consciousness about the new conveyance. Prior to the sale, Crowley's announced a prize for the best essay on the topic "Why are escalators better than elevators?" Over $200 in prizes were awarded to nine persons, with the first prize going to Mrs. Joseph Roman of Port Huron. Mrs. Roman must have been impressed to see the escalators after a formidable sixty-mile journey—quite a distance in 1928!

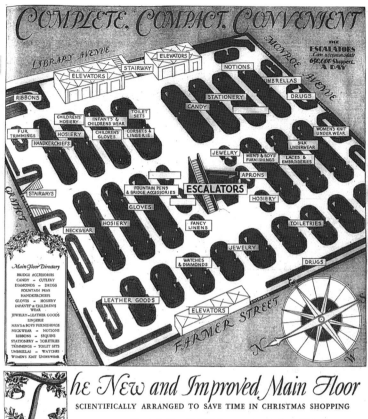

A 1928 ad illustrated the remodeled first floor of Crowley, Milner & Co. Note the famous wooden escalators in the center of the floor. *Collection of the author.*

While the customers were shopping, an informal reception was held in Crowley's executive offices to celebrate the store's nineteenth anniversary and look forward to the improvements yet to come. As the year went on, elements of the improvement program were unveiled one-by-one. A new first floor of glass-and-walnut cases stocked with fashionable merchandise emerged from the dust of construction. Crowley's called it "a glorification

Spaciously Wider Aisles—
More Conveniently Arranged Departments

Make shopping here a profitable pleasure for seekers of high grade as well as medium grade merchandise.

This store meets every advancing demand of Detroit's progress — in larger assortments of better merchandise at Crowley Milner prices.

In fact, the first impression one gets here is the wholesome quality of the merchandise as compared to its low prices.

Our steady increase in good will is due to our policy of quick turnover and small profits.

CROWLEY, MILNER & COMPANY

The spaciousness of the new first-floor arrangement alleviated congestion in the 800,000-square-foot store. *Courtesy of Michael Hauser.*

of the three greatest factors in modern merchandising—Compactness, Convenience and Completeness." The rethinking of the departments on the new floor, consisting of mostly ladies' accessories, jewelry and notions, was made possible by the removal of men's merchandise to the East Building.

Crowley's new mezzanine alleviated congestion in the store and introduced a new tearoom for customers. Later, the shoe department was moved and a beauty salon installed overlooking the first floor. *Collection of the author.*

When the dust cleared, a completely new mezzanine became a much-heralded feature of Crowley's. The new mezzanine housed the store's book, gift and silver departments; it also housed a travel bureau and a completely new tearoom, freeing up space on the fourth floor for more merchandise. Of the Mezzanine Tea Room, as it was called, Crowley's told customers:

> *It's Socially Correct and Altogether Delightful to Have Luncheon, Tea and a Rubber of Bridge in the Mezzanine Tea Room. The sophisticated*

Ladies dine, relax and enjoy conversation in the Mezzanine Tea Room in 1941. The room was originally executed in a cool green color. *Courtesy of the Library of Congress.*

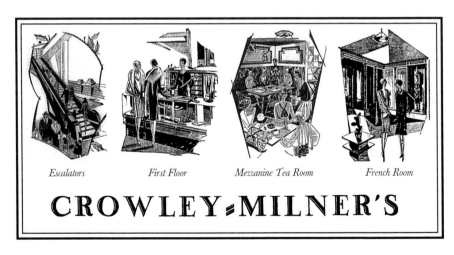

Crowley's enticed customers to come downtown and see the improvements to the store by means of sketches that illustrated the store's amenities. *Collection of the author.*

charm of Art Moderne brings to Crowley-Milner's an atmosphere which smart people appreciate. And the menus, prepared by that superb chef, Henri Gougoltz, formerly of famous Parisian and New York hotels, are tempting to the most blasé appetites. Come in for luncheon or tea—and remain afterward to play bridge. You will find this an easy, pleasant and undeniably smart manner of entertaining your friends.

Later, a revised third floor of fashion shops, including a "Green Room" for sports apparel and a "French Room" that promised fashions "sponsored by the famous Parisian designers Chanel, Patou, LeLong, and others" was presented to Detroit women. About the new fashion shops, the store advertised:

It is something to have coped with the caprices of Paris for nineteen years—watching her every whim…her ever-varying fancies…interpreting the mode authentically, that our Detroit clientele might attain true Parisian chic. And just as the small child celebrates the all-important birthday party in his best bib and tucker…the Fashion Shops prepared with new fittings. The entire Third Floor has taken on a new and luxurious air. Richly soft carpets…shining new cases…everything is conductive to the feeling of well being that accommodates successful shopping. Our fashion Shops are now just as smart as the apparel presented.

Before the end of 1928, Crowley's introduced other improvements, including a remodeled fourth floor (showing shoes, lingerie and children's wear), branch credit offices throughout the store for customer convenience and air cooling provided by a system described by the store as "outside air forced through iced running water…keeps the temperature several degrees cooler than on the street." Yet, after all the newness, so strikingly described, Crowley's went out of its way to assure customers that it still offered the best value to all types of customers, adopting the slogan "It's Clever to be Thrifty" and reminding patrons that "the best way to drive a hard bargain is to buy everything at Crowley-Milner's and know that the price balance is always in your favor."

In fact, Crowley's customers came from many backgrounds, and the store was democratic in nature—that is, other Woodward Avenue stores might turn their nose up at clientele considered below their rank, but Crowley's welcomed all who came to shop there. It was said that the store never ignored what was called "the shawl trade," the less than wealthy women from the

Italian neighborhoods up Gratiot or the Polish wives from Hamtramck, who, as Steven Kennedy remarked, were more likely to wear a babushka than a tiara on their shopping excursions. It was due to these policies of the family-owned retailer that it became known as the "Friendly Store."

Though 1928 was a great year of newness and renewal for Crowley's and the family who owned it, the dark years of the Great Depression loomed only one year ahead. Under Daniel T. Crowley's leadership, however, and despite a sales decline that amounted to three-quarters of the store's 1929 volume, Crowley's was able to struggle through the hard times that hit the nation and industrial Detroit. Crowley's needed a bond issue to provide funds to operate during the Depression, but Daniel Crowley's skill as a financial manager helped the store during these dark times, and it was even able to advance tax payments to the city of Detroit in order to keep it solvent as well. It was during these hard years that Crowley's reputation as a good corporate citizen and benevolent institution was put to the test.

The store did well enough through the Depression that it conducted a memorable contest during the Christmas season of 1932, when twenty-one automobiles were displayed in the store and ultimately given away to as many lucky customers who participated. At the December 27 ceremony awarding keys to the cars, Detroit mayor Frank Murphy thanked Crowley's for the effort, which was designed to promote sales of the city's Depression-wracked auto makers. Speaking to the crowd, general manager James B. Jones said, "By allowing the automobile firms to exhibit their machines here, we felt that we would be helping them to reach a public they could not possibly reach through their showrooms." Winners were escorted down to the main Farmer Street entrance to Crowley's, where the vehicles were lined up for presentation, and the lucky new car owners drove their new rides up Woodward Avenue in a parade, signaling the end of the contest.

If Crowley's and its namesake family did what they could to alleviate the pain of the Great Depression, individuals did their parts, too. As regular as the annual Christmas celebrations in the store were the Depression-era visits by Lowell Turner, who annually brought a group of children from the Protestant Children's Orphanage on East Jefferson Avenue. The children got a tour of the sixth-floor Toyland, a visit to Santa and presents that they probably wouldn't have received if not for the generosity of spirit this man portrayed. Turner, an employee of the Detroit-Michigan Stove Company, was a real-life emissary of Santa Claus whose gifts brightened the holidays

During the Great Depression, Lowell Turner of Detroit annually brought a group of orphaned children to Crowley's to visit Santa and receive a gift. *Courtesy of Michael Hauser.*

of these children and taught all who witnessed his unselfish actions about the true meaning of the Christmas holiday.

In the years before World War II, Crowley's continued operating as a family-owned and oriented store, and though the raw memories of the difficult Depression years began to fade, the store was not completely out of the woods in the 1930s. The last of the Crowley brothers, Daniel T. Crowley, suffered a heart attack and died in his home on April 6, 1936. In addition to Daniel Crowley's skill in leading the store through the Great Depression, a few interesting characteristics of the man were noted in the newspapers: he was an avid curler, served on the advisory board of the Knights of Columbus and the board of directors of the University of Detroit and was a three-term president of Grosse Point Village, where he lived at 203 Lakeland Avenue. His nature, notwithstanding the business savvy he possessed, was perhaps best illustrated by the fact that, out of his own pocket, he provided the city of Detroit with its municipal Christmas tree during the Depression years "rather than see the tradition lost because of lack of city funds," according to the *Detroit Free Press*.

James B. Jones, Crowley's general manager at the time, succeeded Daniel T. Crowley as president of the firm. However, the store continued to operate in the red in spite of its popularity and the respect customers held for the Crowley family and their store. To further consolidate family control in the store, Jenny Crowley purchased all outstanding shares of stock in 1937. As a result, her son, Daniel J. Crowley, who had served as vice-president since 1927, was elevated to president of the store, and even more changes for the future were forecast.

In addition, a bizarre sit-down strike that began on Wednesday, March 10, 1937, brought Crowley's unwanted negative publicity and forced it to close while up to four hundred strikers occupied the building. During the event, executives were allowed in the store but customers were told by striking employees managing the doors that they had better leave "if you don't want to spend the night here!" according to a *Detroit News* article. The company was unable to negotiate with the striking employees because James B. Jones was in Florida on vacation. The strike broke out during the noon rush-hour when restaurant employees on the mezzanine and basement floors refused to serve customers. Most of the remainder of Crowley's three-thousand-plus workforce did not join the strike, though it was reported that some on the main floor did.

Most employees in the East Building departed when the trouble began. By 4:00 p.m., executives ordered all personnel to leave the building, but the strikers stayed overnight while a party atmosphere ensued. The *Detroit News* reported that employees "made merry until after 2 a.m., with two orchestras playing for dancing and girls who had participated in the recent Woolworth Strike putting on a floor show." At the heart of the dispute was a demand by the Chefs, Cooks and Pastry Cooks Union and the Waiters and Waitresses Union for a higher pay scale six days earlier, but in Jones's absence, Crowley's could not take action, let alone negotiate a deal. The Retail Clerks Protective Association had made similar demands but promised not to strike until the president of the company returned.

In fact, the strike was one of a wave of sit-down strikes that hit retailers and larger industrial companies like General Motors during 1937. Scores of still-unemployed workers eager for work caused employees of stores like Crowley, Milner & Co. to believe that their employers were keeping their wages low due to the ease of replacing them, fomenting the strikes. In most cases, police refused to intervene, calling the strikes "private disputes," and though Crowley's remained closed from the start of the strike through the weekend, negotiations that began when president Jones hastily returned to Detroit brought calm, and the store was able to resume "business as usual." Another strike, this time of delivery drivers, affected the store in 1939 but was similarly settled without incident.

Crowley's profitability improved, but by 1939, the store was back in the red. A hasty executive meeting in April 1939 produced a new budget forecast that emphasized cost-cutting, margin increases, improvements to the physical appearance of the store and a wider merchandise selection appealing to a larger client base. In 1940, Crowley's hired Ohio native Jay D. Runkle as vice-president and general manager. Runkle, at the time forty-nine years of age, was educated at Dartmouth and served as a university professor before putting his academic knowledge to use, first in Dayton, Ohio, and later at Crowley's, where he was credited with giving "the store its place among the progressive institutions in the trade," according to a 1949 article in the National Retail Dry Goods Association's publication *Stores*, on the occasion of Runkle's receipt of the group's Gold Medal Award. The article went on to say, "The improved standing of the store is a sweeping demonstration of Runkle's ability to plan shrewdly and bring the planned improvements into being."

Runkle put his former role as a university professor to good use at Crowley's, as he instituted innovative merchandising methods to improve Crowley's bottom line. Known informally as "the Professor," Runkle instituted weekly training sessions in which he taught merchandise managers using a blackboard, chalk and flip charts, demanding that quality, dependability and fashion become the basis for his colleague's decisions.

Crowley's also weathered the war years, sponsoring war bond drives and even opening a Victory Center on the third floor of the East Building with exhibits and an eight-hundred-person auditorium that could be used by volunteer organizations to promote the country's war effort. In addition, the Victory Center hosted war-related exhibits such as the March 1943 program highlighting the "effort of the exiled Netherlands Government in London and the fighting Dutch in their homeland." The exhibit featured a talk by Royal Netherlands Navy commander Johan Geys, who was in town while his submarine was being repaired after a Nazi attack in the North Sea. Geys showed shrapnel-riddled steel plates from his craft and described his service in "whittling down the enemy's supply fleet."

A brutal robbery took place in the store's cash office on January 19, 1943. Nellie Roney, who originally worked for Pardridge & Blackwell beginning in 1908, stayed on through the Crowley transition and rose to the rank of general cashier. She later recalled the event in the fiftieth-anniversary edition of Crowley's *Round Up*, saying, "The holdup man gave me a note signed 'The Shadow' and told me to hand over large bills. I turned and flew to the

CROWLEY'S
The Friendly Store Where It's Easy to Buy

We Proudly Salute
Detroit's Automotive Golden Jubilee
1896 · · · · · 1946

Crowley's, The Friendly Store, Looking From the Downtown Library.
Total Area of 793,934 Square Feet—or 17½ Acres

| IN 1908 | IN 1917 | IN 1920 | IN 1921 |
| Gratiot Front | Gratiot Front | Gratiot Front | Gratiot Fro |

WE believe in great names, *dependable* names. Names that stand for quality of performance and stability. Such are the names we find starred on the pages of the Automotive Industry's magnificent 50 year history. And so today, when all America joins Detroit in celebrating the Automotive Golden Jubilee, we say "hats off" to those great names in the motor industry that have contributed so much to its growth, and have helped it achieve world wide renown.

WE also believe in great names in the world of merchandising. Names that have stood the test of time, names that have justly earned acceptance through character and dependability. Crowley's is proud to share its name with great brand names. Names that have become household words with the American buying public. Names that give complete assurance of fine craftsmanship and service.

On the occasion of Detroit's automotive jubilee year, 1946, Crowley's promoted its rapid but steady growth and its brand-name merchandising policy. *Courtesy of Michael Hauser.*

end of the cash cage. He went through the wicket, and shot Miss Caldwell in the neck, and made off with the bills."

Josephine Caldwell, who began working for Pardridge & Walsh in 1899, had left Crowley's to raise a family in 1914 but returned to the position of head cashier when her husband passed away. Fortunately, her gunshot wound was not fatal, and she made a full recovery. Almost four years later, the Detroit police announced that no one would ever be arrested or brought to trial for the crime because they received notice that William Copeland—who had been arrested for a similar department store holdup in Manhattan, as well as the murder of his wife—admitted to the Crowley heist and shooting in jail. He was electrocuted on December 20, 1946, in Washington, D.C.

After the war, Crowley, Milner & Co. was poised to take advantage of the industrial and economic boom that would increase the wealth of Detroit and the prosperity of its residents. The store had increased its physical plant in 1950 by taking over some adjacent, low-rise properties at the corner of Gratiot Avenue and Broadway. The so-called Crowley's Annex was initially used to house the store's major appliance department, which was growing due to the explosion of new house construction in Detroit.

Jay D. Runkle   *James H. Chamberlain*

Left: Jay D. Runkle, general manager of Crowley, Milner & Co. *Right*: Runkle's successor, James H. Chamberlain. *Courtesy of Michael Hauser.*

Crowley's put itself up to the challenge of the postwar world and resumed its role as one of Detroit's favorite places to shop, though it would always take second place in sales behind the giant and growing J.L. Hudson Company. Jay D. Runkle retired in 1954 and was succeeded as vice-president by James H. Chamberlain, who focused on the baby boom era and helped Crowley's negotiate the changing marketplace of the 1950s. He was aided in his work by able Crowley employees and younger members of the Crowley family who joined the store. These were, of course, Daniel J. Crowley, who remained in his position as president; Katherine Travis, Joseph J. Crowley's daughter, who was vice-president and director of public relations; Joseph and Richard Keys, buyers, both sons of Joseph Crowley's daughter Helen; and his daughter Marjorie's husband, David G. Standart, who was vice-president and branch manager. They gave the store the distinction of being led by three generations of the family whose common goal was to make Crowley's, as its ads proclaimed, "A Great Place to Shop."

8

A GREAT PLACE
TO SHOP

*A*s Detroit spread outward along its radial avenues, its population, flush with cash from high-paying automotive jobs sourced by the postwar industrial boom, led the expansion of the city's retail market. Real estate development boomed as well, creating new neighborhoods all over the city and past its boundaries. The dynamic leadership of Joseph L. Hudson's nephews, the four Webber brothers, soon inspired them to look for growth opportunities for the famously large store named after their uncle. The result was the 1954 opening of Northland, a Hudson's-anchored shopping complex in Southfield, Michigan, northwest of downtown Detroit and just over the city's northern boundary of Base Line (8 Mile) Road. A similar complex had actually been planned earlier, to be located fifteen miles to the east in Harper Woods, Michigan, close to the wealthy enclaves of the Grosse Pointes along Lake St. Clair, but postwar material shortages and the reluctance of local authorities to approve such a large and innovative development delayed its opening until 1957.

Even though these developments drew money away from downtown Detroit, the shopping district remained strong, attracting shoppers to special events like Downtown Detroit Days, designed to increase off-season business at the big stores as well as the smaller shops surrounding them. Crowley's was strong enough that in 1958 it planned a yearlong fiftieth anniversary celebration with a theme of "Fifty Years of Friendliness."

Jenny Crowley, the last active member of the founding generation, passed away on August 18, 1956, surviving her husband by thirty-one years. Until the illness preceding her passing, she had continued her store visits and spry walks through the store to greet clerks. When she cut the cake at the store's forty-fourth anniversary in 1952, a *Detroit News* article in her honor called her "the woman who mothered [Crowley's] growth for 44 years" and said she was looking forward to greater achievements (the store then had about $25 million in annual sales) and planned to keep up her hands-on management style for some years to come. After a funeral mass at St. Peter & Paul Jesuit church on Jefferson Avenue, Jenny Crowley was laid to rest beside her husband in Detroit's historic Mt. Elliot Cemetery.

Jenny Crowley devoted much of her time to the store, from the valuable insights proffered on her regular visits to acting as executor for her late husband's estate. From her childhood through her education at Liggett School and Sacred Heart Convent to her marriage to a successful businessman, Jenny developed a business acumen that helped her lead one of the nation's largest department stores and further the interests of her family. Rather humbly, Mrs. Crowley attributed her success to her "woman's intuition," but the forty-eight years she spent quietly directing progress and offering guidance to executives indicates that it was her knowledge, understanding and pure business savvy that helped build her success in life.

A further loss to the store and the Crowley family occurred on February 10, 1957, when Daniel J. Crowley was found dead in the home he had shared with his mother, at 243 Lakeland Avenue. A caretaker, who was instructed to call one of Daniel's brothers-in-law if he saw anything unusual going on at the house, called to say that the lights were on all night. When John Keys and David Standart entered the house to investigate, they found the sixty-five-year-old Crowley hanging from a rope affixed to the main staircase. Relatives said Crowley "had been ill and despondent" since his mother's death the previous August. His passing left the controlling interest in Crowley, Milner & Co. in the hands of Joseph and Jenny Crowley's three surviving daughters: Mrs. (Helen) John G. Keys, Mrs. (Marjorie) David G. Standart and Mrs. (Katherine) De Hull N. Travis.

Crowley's fiftieth-anniversary year was itself a happy event that spanned the whole of 1958 and celebrated the store's growth and position in the Detroit marketplace. While a large anniversary sale was of necessity the most important event of the year, James H. Chamberlain introduced the yearlong celebration with a letter in the *Round Up*:

> *In 1958, Crowley's will celebrate its 50th Anniversary as a leading department store in the City of Detroit. We intend to make it an outstanding*

Left: Jenny Crowley, wife of Crowley, Milner & Co. founder Joseph J. Crowley. *Right*: Their son, Daniel J. Crowley, president of Crowley, Milner & Co. from 1937 until his death in 1957. *Courtesy of Michael Hauser.*

year. Recently, I had an out-of-town visitor whom I took through our store and through some other stores in the city. As we rode the escalator of a competing store, my guest turned to me and said "Mr. Chamberlain, why should anyone bother to shop at Crowley's?" I've thought about that question many times, and I wish you would think about it, too. Why do customers come here? Is it our prices? Easy shopping? Attractive displays? Assortments? Yes, these things are important, but there must be a more compelling reason. There is, indeed—it's our people—our people and the service they give. Customers expect our prices to be competitive and they expect us to stand behind our goods; but our big advantage lies in a staff of people who are trying to please, and I would emphasize the word "trying." Customers will forgive some mistakes if they know we are making a sincere effort to please them. I am not talking about salespeople. Every person in this store is involved directly or indirectly in pleasing customers—cashiers, elevator operators, packers, porters and maids, telephone operators, etc. All of these jobs are important—there is no such thing as an unimportant job in this store. We are all part of the team and it's a good team, too. We all know that competition for customers is getting keener every year. If 1958 is to be an outstanding year, we must play up our advantage. That means the continued effort of every person to do their job a little better thus pleasing more customers. With all of us working toward this common end, I am sure 1958 will be a very successful year.

In his letter, Chamberlain essentially printed a recipe for the "Friendly Store's" future as it had traditionally developed in the past; indeed, a celebratory article in the February 23, 1958 *Detroit Free Press* was entitled "Crowley's Friendliness Began in '08" and noted that the promises made by the owners in their ad announcing the new Crowley, Milner & Co. fifty years earlier had largely been fulfilled. The article singled out a "girl" at Crowley's stationery counter, one Deanna Lapuszewski, then aged twenty, who obviously fulfilled Chamberlain's ideals when she said, "I like working here; it's a friendly place."

In spite of strong downtown sales, though, there had to be concern on the eighth floor as Crowley's management watched its neighbor, the Ernst Kern Company crumble. In 1957, Otto Kern, son of the seventy-five-year-old store's founder, who purchased his late brother Ernst Jr.'s share of the business in 1953, announced that he was exiting the retail business because "he didn't want the added responsibility of outlying stores, and outlying stores have become a necessity." The announcement puzzled the Kern employees, who had attended a *fête* on the occasion of the anniversary at which Otto Kern stated, "We will operate under the same name we have had through the years and we are not going to sell to anyone."

He had sold his shares to Irving Levick, a New York businessman who had taken possession of Sattler's, Inc., a highly promotional department store that anchored one of Buffalo's ethnic shopping districts. When rumors circulated that Kern's might become a Detroit outpost of Sattler's, Aaron Rabow, a partner of Levick's, denied them. Eventually, Benjamin Goldstein, a former executive of Detroit's Winkelman's women's fashion stores, was announced as Kern's new president. A seasoned merchant, Goldstein began a remodeling program at Kern's that appeared to give the traditional store a new lease on life and hinted that a branch store was very much in Kern's future.

In March 1958, Levick sold his interest in the store directly to Goldstein, who, shortly thereafter, filed for reorganization under federal bankruptcy laws. Frederick F. Davis was appointed Kern's trustee and sold the businesses assets to Louis Krause of Cleveland. Krause was an associate of Leon Schottenstein of Columbus, Ohio, head of a business that, in the future, would be linked with the demise of several of America's most well-known stores. Halle's of Cleveland, Lamson's of Toledo and, as it will be seen, Crowley's itself, would disappear once the Schottenstein organization became involved with the Detroit firm. Kern's was, in hindsight, a predecessor to Crowley's as a victim of involvement with the Schottenstein organization.

After a considerable amount of legal wrangling, Kern's was set to go out of business on December 23, 1959. The *Detroit Free Press* reported in a solemn tone:

> *Mrs. Charlotte Wojnicki is a widow who went into sales work after the death of her husband. She had been at Kern's eight years. "It seemed like it couldn't happen—but here it is, the last day. It's hard to believe." The end has been in sight for several months, and many left during the fall to take other positions. The rest hoped that a miracle would occur. But it didn't. The employees wrote their last sales slips, took a long look at the elegant*

Crowley's in the 1960s as seen from the corner of Farmer Street and Monroe Avenue, with Hudson Tower looming in the background. *Courtesy of Dan Austin.*

Crowley's first branch store was located in the Westborn Center. Though it was not as innovative as Hudson's contemporary Northland and Eastland experiments in shopping center design, its conventional strip-center layout afforded the particularly elegant Crowley store visibility and traffic exposure. *Collection of the author.*

whiteness of the main floor, the delicate chandeliers, and walked slowly out. A lovely part of old Detroit was dead.

Kern's elegant building would be subdivided into small ground-floor shops before its demolition in 1966 in anticipation of a massive urban renewal project that never got off the ground. Crowley's, though, carried on, aware that at least a part of its future would lie in the suburbs.

With Crowley's facing a troubling future, President James H. Chamberlain recognized that the store had to build outlying branches in order to cope with the decentralization of Detroit itself. The prime locations, however, were in possession of its arch-competitor, the J.L. Hudson Company. Both Northland and Eastland were designed as one-anchor, one-stop shopping hubs with enormous Hudson stores consisting of 300,000 to 400,000 square feet of space each, not to mention the large area devoted to smaller stores. Neither offered the physical room or a good location for the type of branch Crowley's could operate successfully. As a result, Crowley's followed its own path in the development of branch stores. It decided on its own locations and merchandised those stores to appeal to the market in which they were located. While this policy ultimately led to Crowley's being in the Detroit market's "secondary" shopping center locations, Crowley's was happy to fill in the need wherever it was located—after all, it was indeed the "Friendly Store."

In March of the anniversary year, press reports announced that a new $5 million shopping center, to be known as Westborn, would be built in

suburban Dearborn, at Michigan Avenue and Outer Drive, with a three-level Crowley's store as an anchor. Westborn marked the beginning of Crowley's move to serve suburban areas directly, but the contrast between Hudson's approach to the same problem could not be more telling. Both Northland and Eastland were massive, self-contained architectural environments, designed by a world-famous architect (Victor Gruen) and developed internally by Hudson's. Westborn was a strip-type center with the new Crowley branch attached.

Ads for the February 26, 1959 grand opening of Westborn Center called it:

> *A magnificent center in a dynamic community. Shopping is a family affair at this complete one-stop shopping center. You'll find repair and service facilities. You'll shop for food! You'll shop for everything from a straight pin to the latest in fashions for yourself, your family, your home! All Roads lead to Westborn!*

The official grand opening, attended by store officials and Dearborn mayor Orville Hubbard, took place outside Crowley's new 106,000-square-foot store. The *Dearborn Guide* reported that the "center has been appropriately decorated with flags and banners for the grand opening, giving it a festive and spring-like appearance even in the middle of a severe winter." There were $2,000 in prizes, live radio broadcasts and strolling clowns to entertain children offered as a part of Westborn Center's inaugural celebrations.

James H. Chamberlain spoke of the significance of the new store to Crowley's:

> *Opening of this new store will mark our first venture outside the downtown area, and it will be our aim to become an important part*

Crowley's Westborn was sheathed in brick and fieldstone, and a colonnade protected shoppers from the rain at the ground floor. The image was taken during the February 1959 grand opening when the buildings were decorated with flags and bunting. *Courtesy of Walter P. Reuther Library, Archives of Labor and Urban Affairs, Wayne State University.*

of the Dearborn community, participating in civic activities as a good corporate citizen should.

He added that the three-level store, with a basement and two floors above ground, would offer the same merchandise and services as the downtown Crowley's and emphasized that Crowley's represented "the highest quality fashion merchandise." Chamberlain also mentioned the top-level auditorium, with kitchen and stage, that had a capacity of two hundred and, he speculated, "would be much in demand by clubs and community groups in the Dearborn area."

The *Dearborn Press* described the new Crowley's Westborn in great detail: "Westborn Built to Keep Shoppers in Detroit—Panorama of Colors, Advanced Styling—Featured in Crowley's Ultra-Modern New Dearborn Store," and its descriptions help create a visual image of what the store looked like over fifty-five years ago. The paper piqued the interest of readers with descriptions of fieldstone-lined vestibules "where customers will find settees for their convenience, placed against ceiling-high screens of louvered panels framed in white against imported silk cloth" and of the ladies' accessory area, where "charcoal grays, accented with white and brass are set against walls covered with imported Japanese grass cloth in pink and beige." Elsewhere on the store's main level were a lingerie shop, gifts and silverware, piece goods and sewing notions and a full-line men's store in a decidedly more masculine style.

Upstairs, shoppers could find ladies' fashion departments arrayed around a central sportswear section. The floor also featured a shoe salon, a millinery section with its own hat bar, children's wear, linens and domestics, along with customer services that the paper described:

> *Madame can also rest and chat with her friends in one of the comfortable lounges, have her hair styled, enjoy a delicious lunch in the beautifully-appointed lunch room and shop some more in a perfectly-blended atmosphere of courtesy, beauty, music and comfort. At the end of Madam's shopping day, she can drive around to the station at the back of the store where all her packages will be gathered together for easy pick-up.*

On the lower level of Crowley's new store, the *Dearborn Press* found a complete home furnishings selection ranging from furniture, rugs and lamps to housewares, hardware and a garden shop. The radio and TV departments included a record bar, and the remainder of the floor housed the store offices and receiving and marking rooms. Throughout the store, the various colors and decorative schemes were tied together by a consistent use of wormy chestnut panels and interior dividers "beautifully hand-decorated by professional artists." The interior design of Crowley's Westborn was executed by Flannery Associates of Pittsburgh, while the exterior, like the shopping center itself, was the work of local architect Ted Rogvoy.

Crowley's first branch store became an unqualified success, serving as it did Detroit's growing western suburbs. Ably managed by Crowley's son-in-law David G. Standart, who grew up in his own family's hardware store, it was the fifty-one-year-old company's first taste of business outside the downtown core.

There wasn't much of a wait for Crowley's to take another bite. On November 6, 1959, store president James H. Chamberlain added that Crowley's had signed a lease for a forty-five-thousand-square-foot branch in Detroit's Grand River and Greenfield Road shopping district. Located at 15270 Grand River Avenue, the three-level structure was previously occupied by the H.L. Green Company, a regional variety store operation that was exiting the Detroit market. Chamberlain announced that Flannery

For its second branch store, Crowley's leased a former variety store in an established shopping area on Grand River Avenue on the west side of Detroit. *Courtesy of Walter P. Reuther Library, Archives of Labor and Urban Affairs, Wayne State University.*

Associates had been hired to renew the building's interior, but due to its smaller size, the new branch would only carry the so-called soft lines of family clothing, shoes, linens, draperies and piece goods.

Crowley's Grand River store opened on March 10, 1960, as its third branch. Located in an established shopping district anchored by JCPenney, Montgomery Ward and local off-price department store Federal's, the branch satisfied Crowley's sales expectations and, in spite of its small size, became an integral part of the store's metropolitan image. Stephen Kennedy did, however, refer to the store as "that dinky little Grand River store" when discussing the difficulty buyers had when merchandising a retailer with a large downtown headquarters and branches of different sizes. Yet the Grand River store, through its neighborhood location and sheer longevity certainly did its job in supporting the notion of Crowley's as the "Friendly Store—Where It's Easy to Shop."

Crowley's early branch stores helped the company address the suburbanization of the Detroit area, even if they were a match in neither size nor location for Hudson's impressive Northland and Eastland stores. The larger store even began to open freestanding budget stores in a few locations and planned new stores in Pontiac and Westland. Crowley's, though, had no presence in the suburbs on the east side. Detroiters, perhaps due to the dividing line of Woodward Avenue as the central spoke in its radial layout, identify themselves strongly with "their" side of town. East-siders regularly become lost on the roads of the opposite side of town and vice-versa. Hudson's carefully spotted its stores around town; when Crowley's looked for alternate sites, it had to take what it could find.

Crowley's Macomb Mall branch, mostly identical to the Livonia Mall store, was essentially a two-story box, but the two-toned brick laid in a Dutch-bond pattern, precast canopies and custom light fixtures gave the buildings detail and character. *Courtesy of Redstone Associates.*

In a few years, though, Crowley's rectified the situation and scored another first. In addition to being the first Detroit store to offer customers time payment plans (through the Industrial Morris Plan Bank), the first to have escalators, the first with a motorized delivery fleet and the first to provide a group health insurance policy for its employees, it became the first department store in Detroit to open twin branches on the same day, October 29, 1964, when the new Macomb Mall and Livonia Mall stores took their places in the Crowley lineup.

Announced by the company in April 1964, the stores were "twins" in practically all respects, as were the shopping malls in which they were located. In actuality, the Macomb Mall location, in Roseville on the east side, was the mirror image of Livonia Mall, located in the eponymous suburb west of Detroit. Externally, the two stores were practically identical, modernistic block-like rectangles executed in light, buff-colored brick with precast concrete canopies at the entries and a one-story hardware and garden shop pavilion off to the side.

The mall entrance to the Macomb Mall Crowley's store featured a halo-illuminated script logo mounted on polished stone panels. The interior layout, based on clear aisles leading from the mall entrance to the front of the store, can clearly be seen. *Courtesy of Redstone Associates.*

Rectangular modernistic interpretations of traditional coach lights mounted on the exposed steel frames of the structure bathed the stores' façades in light, and an illuminated "Crowley's" logo was carried above the entrances on a panel of brown brick in the traditional script that now identified the stores throughout the Detroit metropolitan area. Both the stores and their respective shopping centers were designed by architect Louis Redstone, also a well-known author and a vocal proponent of the integration of fine art into architecture.

Inside, the new stores featured open window display areas between dual entrances that corresponded to twin aisles that led longitudinally across the store to the mall entrance. Between these aisles, counter after counter offered women's cosmetics and accessories, while the women's fashion departments flanked the aisle on one side and menswear the other. An off-center escalator led to the second floor, where furniture, appliances, electronics and a full range of home furnishings were arrayed. Interestingly, and in contrast to competitor Hudson's general practice, the stores both had branches of the downtown basement budget store, unusually located at the back of the second floor, in Crowley's case.

Interestingly, in 1965, Crowley's announced that it would open a branch in the Oakland Mall in the northern suburb of Troy. The development of the mall began with the construction of the largest Sears, Roebuck &

Co. store in the nation at the corner of Fourteen Mile and John R. Roads. Sears duly opened in 1965, and the mall was scheduled to open later, with Crowley, Milner & Co. at the other end of the twin-anchor shopping center. However, the opening expenses of the twin stores at Macomb and Livonia put pressure on Crowley's finances, and the Oakland Mall plan was dropped four months after its announcement. The J.L. Hudson Company opened an enormous, three-floor-and-a-basement branch in the location once coveted by Crowley's in 1968. Until 1978, no Detroit shopping center featured both of the city's big department stores.

James H. Chamberlain stated that the Macomb Mall store fulfilled a need that Crowley's had already recognized, saying, "Macomb county, with a population of young, home-owning adults and growing families, has created a need that Crowley's department store will fill." The *Macomb Daily* referred to the new east side mall as "an entirely new concept in shopping." Indeed, the twin malls were, after the much smaller Pontiac Mall that opened in 1963, among the first enclosed and climate-controlled shopping malls in the Detroit market, Hudson's Northland and Eastland being open-air centers.

In Livonia, the mall and its large new Crowley's store was met with equal praise and approval. The *Observer* singled out Carl Wesebaum, general superintendent of the store, for his contributions in coordinating the work of building not one but two stores over the past year. Wesebaum disclaimed personal credit, saying, "The tremendous teamwork of the entire family of Crowley executives and the countless others who contributed so much, has made the successful completion of the new mall stores in Livonia and Macomb a reality."

Livonia Mall was identical to its eastern sibling, except for the fact that it was a mirror image, with the Crowley's store on the left. *Collection of the author.*

Crowley's full-page ads invited customers to attend the twin grand openings:

> *Bring the whole family to the gala opening…Join us Thursday for the grand opening of an exciting new Crowley's. Every square foot has been planned for your comfort and convenience. You'll like the complete assortments in over 50 departments, including a Budget Store on the second level. MORE for women, MORE for Men, MORE for Children, MORE for your home…plus, MORE of the services and extras you'd expect at Crowley's. We're happy to be here and we'll strive to make you a happy, satisfied customer.*

Within a short five years, Crowley's ringed Detroit with significant suburban stores that addressed competition and the growth of the metropolitan area suddenly rendering a single shopping center downtown an anachronism. However, though diminished, downtown Detroit in this era was still vibrant and full of shoppers and entertainment-seekers. Accordingly, Crowley's downtown maintained its status as the company's flagship as well as its role as an anchor in the only shopping center that featured both of the city's favorite local department stores.

Crowley's downtown was, more than anything else, a fixture; it was a place that customers knew inside and out and expected would always be there. After all, one's parents, and maybe even grandparents, had shopped there. It sat just kitty-corner from Hudson's, and one wonders how many people perused the floors of the bigger store then went and found something more affordable at Crowley's. Liz Wojes, née Swanson—a northern Michigan home decoration blogger whose blog is known as "Infuse with Liz"—remembers some of the old store's details, saying:

> *As a child, my mother would take my sister and me down to Detroit to the Crowley's and Hudson's stores to shop and see the Christmas displays in the early 1960s. In Crowley's, they had these elevators with wire-reinforced glass doors that allowed you to watch the elevators go up and down and I was always fascinated by them! We just rearranged a bedroom at my mother's home and noticed the back of the dresser had the Crowley-Milner name on the back. Our mother (born 1922) grew up on Chalfonte Avenue in a much more innocent time. I'm glad she shared these places with us that meant so much to her before they were destroyed.*

Norine Blake, in her year or two at the Friendly Store, got to know the store well and even found time to wander over to Hudson's to see

The wood-paneled escalators rise from the third floor upward in this view, circa 1940. *From the Manning Brothers Historic Photograph Collection.*

what was there. "Of course," she says, "it was the friendly store. The employees were all friendly. I got to know the store, since I walked from floor to floor picking up time cards. It was at Crowley's that I learned how to get along with people, how to make a sale, and how to properly pack someone's purchase so it looked nice when they got home." Talking about her experience and her responsibilities as a young woman, she adds, "You know, Crowley's helped me get out in public. Before that, I was shy. You couldn't get a peep out of me."

The young Norine developed an opinion about Hudson's, too. "I was used to walking around Crowley's creaky wooden floors, so, after a while, I decided to take a walk over to Hudson's. I went just to see how it was laid out—I didn't want to work there; just to kill a lunch hour." She adds that working at Crowley's involved a fair amount of variety and even a surprise or two. "In the summer, when merchandise managers were on vacation, I got to fill in for them—all over the place—in draperies, misses' dresses, even the marking room. I took a liking to a 'fella' there, but he later left to join the army."

The surprise came when she was working in the sixth-floor toy department. "The manager said, 'I hear your last name is Mitten. Any relation to Joyce Mitten?'" She relates that she met the Crowley's employee with the same last name and found out they were cousins on her father's side of the family, adding, "And you know, I went to her wedding, when she married a guy that worked at Crowley's, too!" Crowley's was apparently a very friendly store! "I actually knew Joe Keys, and in spite of the fact that he was a Crowley family member and a buyer, I went out with him and his wife many times. I only left Crowley's after I married and didn't have to work anymore, but I enjoyed every minute of it!"

Stephen Kennedy arrived at Crowley's during 1965. James H. Chamberlain had passed away and was succeeded by Robert E. Winkel, who joined Crowley's in 1955. After growing up on a Midwest farm and getting a degree from the University of Illinois, Winkel came to Detroit and joined the accounting staff at the Ernst Kern Company. He transferred to Crowley's when Chamberlain laid out his vision for Crowley's suburban growth, igniting in him the desire to direct that very expansion. Winkel was promoted to vice-president in 1960 and assumed the presidency in 1964. "You just could not believe the ethics this guy had," says Stephen Kennedy of Winkel. "He was just a wonderful man, and a great, loyal human being. His wife, Effie, was a great match for him—she was kind, beautiful had a sense of dignity about her that was extraordinary."

Kennedy, like Norine Blake, worked in a number of capacities from his office in Crowley's eighth-floor executive offices.

You know, when I came to Crowley's in 1965, I took note of the rickety old escalator, dated cash registers and snagged carpet. I came to find out

Robert E. Winkel   Robert Carlson

Left: A portrait of Robert E. Winkel in the 1960s. *Right*: Robert Carlson, his successor. *Courtesy of Michael Hauser.*

that the board—though they were genuinely nice people—were older folks who remembered the '29 bank crash. They would have liked to expand the company, but since they didn't really have debt, they were reluctant to borrow. I had even learned that they were offered a place at Northland, Eastland and Westland, but didn't want to borrow in order to make it happen. For a moment, I thought that I wouldn't be able to do anything, but Bob Winkel said, "Oh, yes, you can. You just have to sell the board." So the first thing I looked at was the charge card operation. It was hopelessly antiquated, and the billing was a nightmare, all done by hand. At the time, national credit cards like BankAmericard were just getting started. Security Bank & Trust in Trenton, Michigan, had begun a "billing service" for local merchants, and when I went there, I met future governor John Engler, who asked if the bank could take over our credit operation. So I audited our receivables, and was able to "sell the board" who were worried about the store losing identity on account of a generic credit card. However, it modernized the system and saved the company a ton of money. Afterward, we looked at the payroll system, which was in fact 15 little old ladies stuffing cash into envelopes after taking time cards and calculating everything by hand. I just said to

myself, "What the hell are we doing? This is not only nuts, it's dangerous!"
So we bought payroll machines to streamline the whole process, but I had to
work evenings and weekends to enter the data of 3,000 employees into the
new equipment before it could be put to use. That's how I gained experience
and was eventually named operations manager.

In 1960, the Detroit office of the Veterans Administration (VA) vacated its building on East Jefferson Avenue, which was scheduled to be torn down due to the construction of the Chrysler Freeway. Crowley's entered into a deal with the VA that would lease the first six floors of the East Building and the two-floor annex adjacent to it to the government agency. As a result, the men's store, which had occupied the first two floors of the East Building, moved westward into the Main Building. Robert Winkel stressed, "This move does not in any sense mean a contraction in Crowley's operation in the downtown store, but it does mean that we can provide better service and complete merchandise assortments in an area that will make shopping more convenient for our customers." In reality, it was hard to deny that sales lost to suburban stores made the lease an attractive proposition.

The store got a facelift in the 1960s after the Kern block, with its elegant Kern building and historic Detroit Opera House, was demolished in 1966. Crowley's no longer sat in a dense urban landscape but had a barren open space as its new front lawn. As a result, the management authorized a general face-lifting and cleaning of the newly exposed store, which had become blackened with grime and was now clearly visible from Woodward Avenue.

Inside, too, the store experienced some renewal, with a newly decorated main floor, characterized by modern brass chandeliers featuring large globe lights and a large-scale store directory on the mezzanine front. Its fashion shops underwent renewal, and in the era in which department stores tried to compete with specialty retailers by introducing the "shops-within-a-store concept," Crowley's third floor gained the "Talk of the Town" shop for designer apparel, the "Cosmopolitan Shop" and the "Young Idea" shop for contemporary women's clothes.

For food service, Crowley's offered customers its Mezzanine Tea Room, which was renamed the "Colonial Dining Room" in the 1960s. It also had a Basement Cafeteria and a Snack Bar for customers. Stephen Kennedy remembers the time, after the Mezzanine Tea Room had itself contracted, that Gloria Vanderbilt came to the store to promote her merchandise line. "We had a tiny part of that restaurant partitioned off as an executive dining

The Farmer Street façade of Crowley's suddenly became visible over a long distance when the Kern block was demolished in 1966. *Courtesy of Mike Grobbel.*

Crowley's interior was refreshed in the 1960s, with new chandeliers, updated fixtures and a large-scale floor-by-floor directory on the mezzanine face. *Courtesy of Walter P. Reuther Library, Archives of Labor and Urban Affairs, Wayne State University.*

room, and we had lunch served there. It was embarrassing, actually, but she was a gracious, delightful lady, and she put everyone at ease."

Christmas at Crowley's during this era was quite special as well. Though Hudson's certainly put the weight of its huge organization into its holiday celebrations, from the nationally known parade to the Christmas fantasyland it created annually on its twelfth floor, Crowley's made the holiday its own in a special way. In 1952, the store introduced the "Santa Graf," a photography service that provided parents with a picture of their children with Old Saint Nick. Also, Crowley's set up an indoor Christmas carnival in the East Building that featured six amusement rides for small children. Aside from elaborate decorations in the store and on its façade and marquee (including a nativity scene), Crowley's breakfast with Santa was introduced and became a Christmas tradition in the East Building's seventh-floor auditorium.

Many residents of Detroit recall downtown shopping at Christmas or even at other times of the year, like Rod Hartwig, who says:

I went on the bus to Crowley's circa 1965 to see the Scholastic Art Award exhibition that was held every year and displayed at Crowley's. My friends

Handsome window displays shaded by a marquee were familiar on the streets around Crowley's while the store was in operation. *Courtesy of Mike Grobbel.*

A night shot of Crowley's, that appeared in the December 1966 issue of *The Big "C,"* the employee newsletter that succeeded *Round Up*, shows the store's nativity scene and holiday lighting set up on the marquee. *Courtesy of Michael Hauser.*

Downtown shoppers could always count on stylish window displays in Crowley's windows, which extended around three sides of the Main Building, as shown in 1968. *Courtesy of Mike Grobbel.*

and I enjoyed exploring the stairwells on various floors and enjoyed the views from all sides of the building. We were in junior high and felt adventurous and looked forward to exploring downtown further. Along with visiting the annual Christmas display at Hudson's a few times when younger, and riding the bus downtown with my mom, these are great memories. I still enjoy going downtown to the Fisher Building tour and others, but still miss the old department stores, sadly a thing of the past.

At other times of the year, Crowley's downtown participated in the Downtown Detroit Days event (one year donating a fur coat as a prize) meant to promote downtown retail sales, held seasonal fashion sales and promotions and annually held a downtown "Women's Day" to pay tribute to the Federation of Women's Clubs of Metropolitan Detroit.

In the first half of the 1960s, downtown may have experienced a decline in sales, but it remained a popular place nonetheless. In 1957, Crowley's *Round Up* featured an article written in cooperation with the Central Business District Association that outlined the many improvements and developments downtown that pointed to "a bright future indeed" for Detroit, according to the author.

Ten years later, though, that future would be clouded in smoke.

9

(A HUNK'A) BURNIN' LOVE

*I*n the early hours of Sunday, July 23, 1967, a police raid on an unlicensed drinking establishment in inner-city Detroit sparked a riot that lasted almost a week and was finally ended after the National Guard and army units were deployed to bring an end to the violence. When the rioting, looting and murder ceased, the statistics were staggering: 43 people were dead, almost 1,200 were injured and two thousand Detroit buildings were burned.

The greatest victim was the city of Detroit. What had been considered a progressive town with a bright future became a place of shame and ruin overnight. The long-term effects were perhaps the most damaging. Traditional residents sought ways to get out of the city that they no longer believed to be safe, and businesses followed them. Shopping crowds downtown diminished after the riot. Commuters felt unsafe traveling through riot-affected areas or found the crumbling atmosphere downtown ominous. After the riot, well publicized crimes like the murder of a Hudson's salesperson in the store itself during a robbery attempt did little to build shoppers' confidence in the downtown district. Events like the annual Christmas tree lighting and Downtown Detroit Days continued but did little to stem the tide that eroded the downtown area's role as the premier retail and entertainment destination. Newer, larger and more elaborate shopping centers across the city line took up the slack.

Crowley's felt the change acutely. "After the riots, downtown sales just dropped and it was obvious that no one was coming down there anymore," says Steve Kennedy, who witnessed the riot's effects firsthand.

The Monday after the riot started, Bob Winkel didn't want to close the store—though he did have his wife and kids sent out of the city for safety's sake—but when I came downtown, all I saw were rifles and shotguns. The salespeople became petrified as the day went on, and Bob finally agreed, telling everyone to "do what you have to do to protect yourself and your family," and most of us left until the conflict was over. Afterwards, Joe Hudson and Henry Ford II formed New Detroit, Inc. in order to help people and prevent that kind of thing from ever happening again. Bob Winkel asked me to serve on it, and I couldn't believe what I saw. We went out into the city and talked with people, and it was discouraging. I saw women living in fleabag hotels with five kids, and all they could tell me that no one gave a damn about them; they couldn't even get their kids into school. While the whole effort was built on good intentions—Joe Hudson and Jerry Cavanaugh [Detroit's mayor at the time] *had great integrity—I just didn't see any help getting out to these people. There was a lot of paperwork, a lot of talk, and no shortage of speech-making. So, having done what I could, I told Bob Winkel that I felt it was time to quit and focus on our business and he agreed.*

That business was a victim of the new reality after the riots of 1967. Not only did revenue decline, but costs increased as the store aged, and in-house crime skyrocketed as well. After Kennedy helped modernize many of the store's systems, he turned his attention to security in order to see if he could improve the situation.

I decided to just watch what was going on closely, and it didn't take long to see what was happening. Of course, there was crime in the outlying stores—a security gal was stabbed making a shoplifting arrest at Macomb Mall, and in Livonia, a Brink's armored car hold-up outside our store resulted in a gun battle and an escaped robber—but downtown, it was chronic. I saw a woman "wobbling" down one of the main floor aisles, and we stopped her on a hunch. Would you believe it, she tried to make off with a portable TV, between her thighs and under her skirt! More disheartening was the staff crime we uncovered. We noticed someone picking up merchandise without a receipt, and were able to uncover a racket involving salespeople, the package-pickup employee, and so-called customers, to get merchandise out of the store without paying for it. Then, when planning to modernize our phone system, we found that employees were making long-distance calls to Washington, D.C., and down south on our dime—but in reality the cost to Crowley's was huge.

Rumors circulated in Detroit about Crowley's closing. Its interiors seemed worn and tattered in comparison with the face-lifted and more glitzy Hudson's on the other side of Farmer Street. In reality, Hudson's remodeling was predicated on contracting floor space in order to save money to combat the same types of losses Crowley's experienced. Among Detroiters who had experienced the glory days downtown, there was a feeling that while Crowley's might slip away, Hudson's would "always be there."

Once Crowley's new "twin" branches became established and began to perform well, the store's bottom line improved in spite of the losses downtown. Having backed out of the Oakland Mall opportunity in 1965, Crowley's began to look for other expansion possibilities. "What do you do in a situation like that?" asks Steve Kennedy. "Well, you buy Demery's, of course!"

Demery's, Inc., was a three-unit department store chain that was founded in 1911 when Michael Demery, who emigrated in 1898 at age twenty-two from Cork, Ireland, assumed the premises of Hook's Dry Goods on Woodward Avenue and Milwaukee Street, in the "Boulevard District," for his own store. Advertising itself as "Detroit's Uptown Department Store," Demery's prospered as the neighborhood developed into the so-called New Center with the construction of General Motors' huge headquarters building and the Art Deco Fisher building on the nearby streets. Demery's opened a three-story addition next to the old store in 1929 to accommodate its success in the neighborhood. Not long after Saks Fifth Avenue joined the neighborhood by opening a store in the Albert Kahn–designed New Center Building in 1940, Demery's replaced its original quarters with a gleaming, streamlined store of its own that opened on November 15 of that year. Demery's advertised that:

Tomorrow, Friday, marks the beginning of a glorious new chapter in Demery's history. When our doors open at 9:30, a new and greater Demery's will be unveiled—a monument to the vision and the courage of Michael Demery, who—28 years ago—went shopping for a likely corner and found it here at Woodward and Milwaukee. From the humble "corner dry goods store" of 1912, Demery's has come far—to take its place in the front rank of Detroit's major retail stores. Pioneered by Demery's, the Woodward-Boulevard section has become the heart of this great city. And here today, more readily accessible to more people than any other store in Detroit, Demery's has almost completely transformed itself—to increase its usefulness to all Detroit—to serve you better.

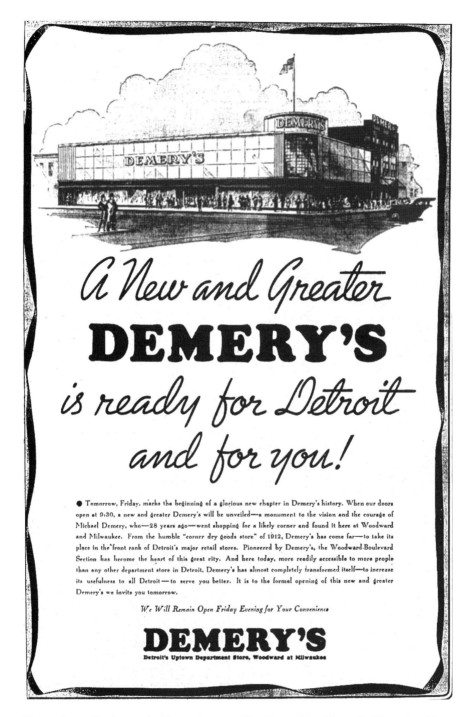

Demery's was clearly proud of its modern new flagship, as this ad from the November 15, 1940 *Detroit News* shows. *Collection of the author.*

In 1955, Detroit businessman John W. Butler, who began at Demery's as a stock boy and later founded Michigan National Bank, purchased the store. Under his leadership, Demery's expanded, opening two branches (both larger than the New Center flagship) in the 1960s. Demery's announced the construction of a branch in suburban Birmingham's downtown shopping area on the corner of Woodward Avenue and Hamilton Street. When the store opened on April 27, 1961, it was hailed as an ideal example of a modern retail store, with open display windows protected by a second-floor overhang, a rear entry approached from a landscaped garden and an open escalator well filled with a large, custom chandelier.

Charles A. Peck, president and Butler's partner in Demery's, said of the sixty-nine-thousand-square-foot store:

> *We actually built it at the corner of Neighborly Avenue and Faith Street. The Neighborly side is bringing the first full-sized department store to the Birmingham community, and we certainly had faith a block long to build and open a $3 million store in the present economy. It is the culmination of long planning, first the intensive search for the right location, where the new Demery's would become an integral part of a complete, dynamic, growing business section; then building a store in the finest concept of architectural beauty and modern design, combining rare beauty of color and imaginative fixtures and lighting, with the newest conveniences for making shopping a pleasant and relaxed experience.*

Four years later, Demery's came to the Detroit suburb of Farmington on August 22, 1965, when it opened an eighty-five-thousand-square-foot store in the Demery's Plaza at the corner of 12 Mile and Farmington Roads. Later, the plaza was renamed Kendallwood, after the planned area in which it was located. Designed by Birmingham architect Clifford Wright, the store's second floor was sheathed in exposed aggregate panels in white, with gold-colored aggregate denoting the store's entrances below. The *Farmington Observer* described the new store and noted "several innovations in retail store design," including what it called the store's focal point, a central escalator court with a sixteen-foot-high chandelier visible from all three of the store's levels. Another innovation was an adjacent S&H Green Stamp showroom. At the time, the store gave away stamps with purchases and provided a spacious and handsome place for customers to redeem them.

Demery's was up for sale due the failure of John W. Butler's other department store investments, Wurzburg's of Grand Rapids and

Collage of the three Demery's stores Crowley, Milner & Co. purchased. *Top*: New Center, Detroit. *Middle*: Birmingham. *Bottom*: Farmington. *Courtesy of Keith D. Butler, Cranbrook Management.*

Arbaugh's of Lansing. Butler's son, Keith, himself an accomplished businessman in the Detroit area, said, "Those were not one of my dad's best investments." On March 12, 1972, the *Detroit News* reported that Crowley's had purchased the three Demery stores and would close them in the middle of May in anticipation of a late-summer reopening after major renovations. The article quoted President Robert Winkel as saying, "The addition of this new space to our present five-store operation provides Crowley's with needed expansion in rapidly developing suburban marketing area, and at the same time allows Crowley's a unique opportunity to show its faith in the vitality and appeal of the Detroit and New Center area."

Winkel's remarks bear out Steve Kennedy's statement that the downtown store had been hurting since the 1967 riots and that shoppers in the Detroit area were abandoning downtown for the suburbs. Ominously, a report in the same paper five weeks later announced that Crowley's was planning to reduce the size of its operation downtown. Robert Winkel explained the contraction, saying, "The downtown building is now too large and inefficient for the sales volume to be expected in the foreseeable future." Winkel also stated that Crowley's was negotiating with the main store's landlord in hopes of retaining a Crowley's store downtown, but if an agreement could not be concluded (Crowley's owned the smaller East Building but leased the main store), Winkel said, "We hope to reach an early agreement as to our termination costs." The writing was on the wall.

At the former Demery's stores, renovations were completed and an opening date of was set for August 3 for the New Center and Farmington Crowley stores. Construction delays postponed the Birmingham opening until August 14. All of them were opened in conjunction with a "Lifestyles '72" promotion. The stores, which eschewed Crowley's lines of hard goods (primarily furniture and appliances) due to the space limitations of the smaller Demery's branches. The opening ads said:

> *A totally new reflection of your lifestyle is ready to come alive! And, it comes to you in an atmosphere charged with appealing innovations. We kept super graphics in mind with generous use of modern color. We utilized fixtures designed for visibility; arranged our departments for simple selection. We looked at your '72 image, projected it in this season's fashions, home and decorator ideas, gifts, housewares and small appliances.*

Crowley's smaller stores, with their limited merchandise range, seemed to point toward the store's future, but before that future would reveal itself, the devastating news that steadfast downtown shoppers, not to mention Crowley's employees, feared became reality on April 18, 1973, when Crowley's president Robert Winkel announced that the department store would phase out operations downtown by 1976. He said that Crowley's lease on the building was set to expire in 1976, and the store would seek a location for a new downtown branch in the interim. The news caused a

Even though the store was facing closure, customers delighted in a ride on the wooden escalators, a now-lost historic artifact. *Courtesy of Dan Austin.*

panic among employees, and the store's executive team circulated through the floors in order to reassure them that their jobs were not in danger. The newspapers prophesied that the announcement that Crowley's would close the location it occupied since 1908 was actually good news. They speculated—in hindsight without evidence—that a new Crowley's store would signal the rebirth of the declining downtown shopping district, citing the 1962 destruction of the Majestic Building for the new headquarters of First Federal Savings and Loan of Detroit as a "good swap." Robert Winkel simply stated, "The building's life has been spent. There is a place for a downtown store, but it should be run as a branch rather than a central organization. Downtown will never again be *the* marketplace, the kingpin of marketplaces in the city."

Before the projected closure downtown occurred, Crowley's became the first retailer to open at Lakeside Mall, a new development in suburban Sterling Heights on September 11, 1975. Steve Kennedy recalls riding in a private airplane over the site of the new regional shopping center, which was literally out in the cornfields and apple orchards of Detroit's northernmost suburbs. "What Bob Winkel and I noticed, was, though, that all the houses leading up to the site had swimming pools. We had to stop all the chatter and get up there if we wanted to capture those customers! Sears and Penney's were going in there, and we just knew that something good was going to happen at Lakeside."

Literally "out in the country," the new mall was, at the time, beyond the built-up area of the northern Detroit metropolitan area, and Crowley's went it alone until the whole shopping center opened in 1976. Suburbanites drove out to the store to see what was new and liked what they saw. This was Crowley's first "from the ground up" store in over eleven years, and it stood in contrast to its siblings, which were looking dated. The store's exterior was executed in a rich brown brick, slightly lighter than the rest of the mall building, that made the most of a simple modern aesthetic. Inside, intimate sales spaces were connected to one another by wide arches, and the whole interior was executed in warm, rich colors. Overall, the quietly elegant new design was a revelation for Crowley's customers.

When the announcement to close the historic downtown store was made, Robert Winkel warned that the building would be demolished after the store closed; Crowley's lease on the Main Building called for it to be pulled down within six months of its termination. Crowley's owned the building but leased the land from, among others, the Real Estate Investment Trust of America in Boston (remember the Boston upper crust who financed the deal to build the new Pardridge & Blackwell store in 1906?). Even though

Crowley's
in Lakeside Mall
Sterling Heights

Crowley's 1975 Lakeside Mall store had a low-key brick exterior and a lovely interior that pointed to an upscale new direction for the sixty-seven-year-old store. *Collection of the author.*

Crowley's owned the East Building, Winkel said that "planning for the two buildings has to be the same."

In August 1976, Crowley's announced that a new building would be built in suburban Troy, Michigan, to house Crowley's executive offices. Within two months, though, the contracts with architects and contractors for the planned headquarters were abruptly cancelled. The word from Crowley's was "previous plans to move from the city have been deferred because of the current business climate in this market area" and that the executives would be housed in a refurbished East Building. The announcement of a stay of execution for the East Building sparked rumors that the two-building complex would be saved, but Robert Winkel dispelled them, saying that the plan to upgrade the East Building for offices did in no way mean that there was a "change in the status of the downtown store."

Back downtown, the old store continued to deteriorate as maintenance was deferred due to the projected closing. Faded, torn carpeting was patched with duct tape, but the old escalators continued to run. They had become a maintenance nightmare, according to Steve Kennedy. Yet customers, admittedly fewer of them all of the time, wandered through the store, many thinking that perhaps something would be done to keep the store open. It was not to be, however. After the Christmas shopping season of 1976, the president came down to the first floor to speak with employees when the store was in the midst of its regular January clearance.

What he had to say can't have pleased anyone who hoped that the store could somehow be saved. The store would shut its doors on July 2, 1977, after a major liquidation sale, and demolition would begin shortly thereafter, since Crowley's was obligated to turn a clear site back to its landlord by July 1, 1978. Winkel explained that the losses resulting from the downtown store were more than the seventy-year-old company could bear, saying:

> *The continuing decline in sales downtown has resulted in an operating loss that we in no way could continue. In fact, Crowley's losses for the previous year were primarily as a result of the downtown store's operation, but it was exacerbated by losses at Macomb Mall and Westborn due to the opening of the nearby Lakeside and Fairlane Town Center Malls, respectively. It was a perfectly hopeless situation.*

Included in Robert Winkel's remarks on that January day were plans for the 450 employees who would no longer work downtown after July 2. Of these, it was estimated that 150 would retire due to their age, and the others would be offered jobs at other Crowley locations. A total of 400 employees would remain at the new headquarters in the East Building. Stephen Kennedy remembers working in the East Building before it, too, was demolished in 1982. "You wouldn't believe what it was like to watch that wrecking ball bang away at the old store across the street. I'll tell you right now that the whole place shook every time that thing took out another chunk of that old place!"

As the closure date for the downtown store neared, the reality of what it all meant for shoppers, especially those who considered Crowley's "their store,"

Above: The winter months of early 1978 were bleak indeed as downtown workers and the few remaining shoppers watched the destruction of the gracious Crowley, Milner & Co. store on Farmer Street. *Courtesy of Michael Hauser.*

Left: The East Building was not spared the fate suffered by its bigger neighbor after Crowley's moved to a new headquarters outside downtown in the early '80s. *Courtesy of Dan Austin.*

began to set in. Katherine Travis, who had retired as vice-president of public relations in 1960, paid one last visit to her father's store and, along with brother-in-law David G. Standart, greeted familiar employees one last time. It was a bittersweet moment, and as reported by the *Free Press*, the talk turned from good memories of customers, sales and operations to an impromptu critique of what went wrong. Mrs. Travis, a graduate of Vassar College, called Crowley's merchandise "mass-produced and not very fashionable," saying, "It used to be that there was no attempt to establish an image. For his part, David Standart agreed. "It was a very irregular type of operation. You had the fashion—very high fashion—merchandise, and next to it would be very cheap goods. No continuity," he stated.

Leigh Morrison, daughter of Patricia Ann Standart, remembers the Crowley family well at this time, even though she grew up in Tennessee. "I never even knew my grandmother Marjorie, as she passed away when I was very young, but I do have fond memories of visiting Detroit and my grandfather's house. My great aunt Kitty [Katherine Travis] was a very sweet and upscale woman. I can remember her trying to get me to sit still as a child, as she attempted to paint my brother and me." Speaking of her aunt Joann (Standart) Cousino, who served on Crowley's board of directors, she says, "Aunt Judy is a compassionate woman with much strength; we correspond via e-mail quite regularly."

When July approached and the liquidation sales had cleared the store of merchandise, the cavernous interior became a place of remembrance and, it has to be said, worry about the future. Soon-to-be redundant salespeople reminisced about their work and about customers they had encountered in the course of their jobs. Many employees and even some last-minute customers admitted that watching the long-established store wind down was "trying," according to last-day press reports, and they added that seeing the store meet the wrecking ball would "probably be worse."

Meet the wrecking ball, it did, unfortunately. For the rest of the year, and into 1978, piece by piece, the store crumbled and fell to the ground. The demolition works, executed by All-State Wrecking of Mt. Clemens, Michigan, began with the iconic bridge structure over Library Street that framed a view between Crowley's two buildings for generations of shoppers in downtown Detroit. The removal of the bridge allowed modernization work to begin on the East Building while the rest of the store came down. Throughout the brutal Detroit winter, people downtown witnessed the crumbling of the handsome old building and its luxurious Neo-Renaissance details, characterized by the *Detroit News* as "a graceful, columnar, eight-story edifice."

Downtown workers and remaining shoppers, who were now confined to Hudson's and a few other retailers remaining on Woodward Avenue, watched the painful transformation of a familiar, even beloved, building into an asphalt parking lot. The more restrained East Building quietly served as Crowley's headquarters, though the reflective glass block used to close up display windows along the sidewalk gave the once open and popular building an unwelcoming air. Within five years, even Hudson's exited downtown. The area had become unrecognizable to the shoppers who frequented the center of a city once considered truly exceptional and one of the best and most beautiful in the nation. For the foreseeable future, the holes like that left by the demolition of Crowley's would further erode the city's character and obscure memories of its past.

The elimination of red ink caused by Crowley's downtown store resulted in better financial results toward the end of the 1970s. Crowley's was even able to open a few new locations to better serve customers in the suburbs. When the chain of Federal's department stores failed, it left many vacant stores around town, some in undesirable areas. However, two of the best were picked up by

The smallish Arborland store of 1980 was built when the 1960s-era shopping center was enclosed. Unable to compete with nearby regional mall Briarwood, it went off price in 1983, and Crowley's pulled out. *Collection of the author.*

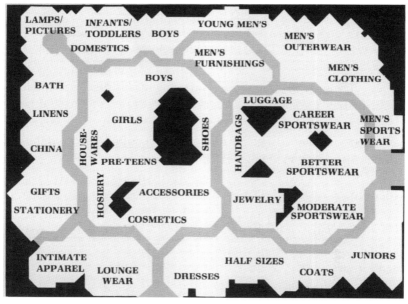

Crowley's Universal Mall store occupied a vacated Federal's department store, but its interior design was an award winner. It quickly became one of the biggest producers in the chain. *Collection of the author.*

Crowley's. A 46,000-square-foot space in the 1961 Arborland shopping center in Ann Arbor became a Crowley's branch as the open-air center was itself being enclosed and upgraded. Closer to Detroit, the Federal's location in the 1965 Universal City shopping center, also remodeled and rechristened as Universal Mall, reopened as a 102,000-square-foot, one-floor Crowley's store in late 1980.

The design of the store's interior, executed by retail specialists John Greenberg Associates (JGA), was praised by trade magazine *Visual Merchandising* and won the 1981 Store Interior Design Award sponsored by the Institute of Store Planners and the National Association of Store Fixture Manufacturers. The interior, crafted in rich colors of chinchilla gray, taupe, plum and beige, was notable for its winding racetrack layout that allowed customers to view merchandise assortments from a variety of angles as they walked through the store and for the fact that such positive results were achieved on a restrictive budget and schedule.

These new stores were important because they pointed toward Crowley's future, away from the center of Detroit, as well as its drifting away from being a traditional full-line department store. Its style and selections began to look more like that of upstart fashion retailers Mervyn's or Kohl's (which came to Detroit by purchasing Federated Department Stores' failed Main Street chain), offering expanded fashion lines and soft goods for the home along with limited housewares selections. The change in Crowley's set the stage for the turbulent years ahead that would end with the store's demise.

10

DETROIT'S OWN
DEPARTMENT STORE

*T*he 1980s may have looked like new era for Crowley's, but it was tinged with nostalgia for the store's downtown glory days. Crowley's had indeed changed, as Detroit itself had, but from time to time, the idea of a new Crowley's store downtown and the ongoing store in the New Center area shined a brief ray of light on the future of retailing in the Motor City. However, that future would lie primarily in the suburbs as the population continued to move outward and the city's tax base and population left as well.

These years saw the end of Robert Winkel's tenure as Crowley's president, though, upon his retirement in 1984, he remained on the store's board of directors for a number of years. Steve Kennedy characterizes the era as one in which he and other Crowley executives "saw our usefulness beginning to slip away," even though it would be years before the store dropped off the local retail map. One thing that dropped off quite quickly was the East Building. The city of Detroit offered to buy it, and Crowley's went looking for a new headquarters.

It found one in 1979 on West Lafayette Boulevard, where a former Greyhound bus maintenance facility became available, and Crowley's took the bait, first renovating the offices and creating a distribution center at the location. The move occurred swiftly over one weekend, but Steve Kennedy said that, as vice-president of operations, he had to deal with complications. "We had an older staff," he remembers, "and as a hands-on, people kind of guy, I realized that the best thing I could do was to protect our employees' jobs. We made that move and retrained people who didn't necessarily have a place in the new building so that they could keep on working for us."

Another problem stemmed from the closure of the downtown store. Kennedy says, "In the old place, buyers' offices were right on the floor adjacent to the departments they bought for. They could talk to salespeople and customers. The whole place was like a laboratory, and that's how they became good at their jobs." With a main office and warehouse remote from the retail sales themselves, buyers became isolated from the store's business, "and that made their job more difficult. Buyers had trouble making the right decisions and merchandise had trouble moving through the company."

Crowley's began to rely on emerging computer systems for help with the complexities of late-twentieth-century retailing, but that, too, had its own problems. Kennedy explains: "Systems today are far, far better and more user friendly. What we had just spit out stacks of data on perforated paper, and that was sheer overkill. Our computer people were smart as hell, but they were not merchandisers. It was hard to tailor the systems to our immediate needs."

One other problem Kennedy mentions involves operations and dealing with authorities. He explains:

> *I don't want to mention the store or the people involved since they might still be in positions where they could be affected. When we were opening a particular store, we applied to the fire marshal for our formal certificate of occupancy, who has final jurisdiction over such things. The store was completely ready and stocked with merchandise, and it was a day or two before the grand opening. The guy brought his wife along as he inspected the store, and when we met with him afterward, he mentioned that she liked a suite of furniture on display. I told him that it would be on sale on opening day, but he persisted and said how much his wife liked it and wanted it. I repeated myself and he told me in no uncertain terms that he expected that furniture or else we would have difficulty getting our certificate of occupancy. I told him I would talk to upper management, and again, Bob Winkel demonstrated his true integrity. He told me, "We are not going to be a part of that. Once it starts, it never ends." We refused and were forced to add additional sprinkler heads at the fire marshal's insistence, even though we know that the store, as built, satisfied all applicable codes. It just goes to show what we dealt with!*

Crowley's hit another snag in 1983 when the owners of Arborland Mall decided to take the shopping center down market and focus on discount retailers. The action left Crowley's in an isolated position, so the store pulled out in May after only three years of operation. Eventually, the mall itself was demolished and replaced with big-box retailers.

When Robert Winkel retired in 1984, Crowley's found a replacement in Robert Carlson, who had come to Detroit in 1978 from Marshall Field & Company of Chicago. He took a position with Crowley's as senior vice-president of merchandising and publicity. Previously, he had spent four years at Field's subsidiary, the well-known and very sophisticated Halle Brothers Co. of Cleveland, Ohio. A deeply religious man, Carlson served as chairman of Faith Covenant Church of Farmington Hills during his time in the Detroit area, and in a *Detroit Free Press* article, Steve Kennedy described him as "a caring, concerned-with-people kind of guy—a hell of a nice man. He's extremely positive and infuses the organization with the belief that we can do anything."

Press interviews with Crowley's new president bore out Kennedy's comments. Carlson mentioned that Crowley's would of necessity change, but it would not "throw the baby out with the bath water—Crowley's will still be Crowley's" and that he was proudest of the fact that the store went through the traumatic closure of its downtown flagship without one employee forced out of the company. Even at this late date, Crowley's was a very benevolent employer—for instance, the company paid benefits to full-time employees and defined full-time as twenty-two and a half hours of work per week.

Soon after Carlson's appointment, things began to happen, and the indication was that Crowley's began to shed its old-fashioned image. Soon, store displays were upgraded in the fashion of Carlson's former employer, with clothes displayed on oversize, torso-like hangers bearing a refined, new Crowley's logo embossed in gold. Store interiors were upgraded, and there was even talk of a new downtown store again, fueled by comments from city officials who were looking to revive at least a part of the failed Cadillac Square mall project.

Carlson based his program for Crowley's future on the store's standing with the public and the vendors with which it dealt, saying, "We have good locations and great employees. We pay our bills. Boy, do we pay our bills! We treat people like ladies and gentlemen." Sales and profits rose to record levels in 1985, and the year was characterized by the opening of a new Crowley's store in the older Tel-Twelve mall in Southfield. The fifty-seven-thousand-square-foot store was carved out of existing lease space and was Crowley's first new store in five years. As the first to open under Carlson's tenure as Crowley's president, it had an upscale design (again planned by local retail

The main mall entrance facing Telegraph Road of Tel-Twelve Mall was modified when Crowley's joined the shopping center in 1985. The store occupied space at the back of the mall. *Courtesy of Michael Lisicky.*

specialists JGA) that well demonstrated the direction Carlson planned for the seventy-seven-year-old retailer.

That year, Crowley's began planning an eleventh store, which, like the failed Arborland branch, was located outside the Detroit area, this time in suburban Flint, Michigan, where the older Eastland shopping center was to be redeveloped. On July 18, 1985, Crowley's announced that it would replace the New Center store it had operated for thirteen years with a new one in the retail gallery of the 1983 New Center One complex across Second Avenue from the landmark Fisher Building on Grand Boulevard. In November, a new store in suburban Westland was announced as well. Downtown, Crowley's looked into the vacant Hughes & Hatcher building on Woodward Avenue as a possible location for a new downtown store, but it was deemed too cramped for Crowley's operation.

Before the three new stores opened, though, Crowley's seemed to become a takeover candidate. A group of investors from Birmingham, Michigan, announced in June 1985 that it was seeking to acquire Crowley, Milner & Co. The news was fairly sensational at the time, but the Crowley heirs were essentially silent about selling their family's store. The offer to buy Crowley's never gained traction and was dropped within a few weeks.

Crowley's moved out of the former Demery's store in Detroit's New Center area and into the contemporary New Center One building across from the large General Motors headquarters building on Grand Boulevard north of downtown. *Courtesy of Marcy Goldstein of JGA.*

Flush with increased profits and looking toward a future it felt would be full of positive growth and expansion, Crowley's opened the first of its new branches on August 11, 1985, at the renamed Courtland Center in Flint. The shopping center was redeveloped by Forest City Enterprises of Cleveland, Ohio, where a former Woolco store was subdivided into mall area, smaller shops and a sixty-one-thousand-square-foot Crowley's store. Crowley's had already shed its furniture, appliance, drapery, fabric and stationery departments, making a smaller, one-story building ideal for its needs as a specialty fashion retailer.

The August 18 opening of the New Center One store was hailed in Crowley's publicity with a slogan that announced "Great Detroit Shopping Is Back! Right in the Center of Everything." The grand opening was more elaborate than the one in Flint, with a crowd of Crowley's "associates" and other New Center workers forming a human chain between the old and new stores in order to pass a symbolic key from old to new, where Robert Carlson led spectators up a red carpet and cut a gold ribbon to open the forty-five-thousand-square-foot, two-level store. Gift certificate prizes were hidden in fortune cookies distributed to customers, and four hundred people lined up to meet former Baltimore Oriole pitcher Jim Palmer, who signed autographs in the store's underwear department. A brochure illustrating the store's location and layout proclaimed:

> *Detroit's New Center is one of America's most dynamic, on-the-go business areas. Over 10,000 people work in ten different buildings connected by glass enclosed skywalks. There's always something going on. Great shopping and restaurants in the General Motors and Fisher Buildings along with exhibits, fashion shows, gallery openings, concerts and theater…all year long. Woodward, Grand Blvd., the Lodge, Ford and Chrysler Freeways all service the area. Complimentary parking is available, just ask for details when you make a purchase. The Shops of New Center One…The Center of Everything!*

Later in the year, the opening of a new, fifty-eight-thousand-square-foot branch in Westland at the redeveloped Wildwood center was a more low-key affair, though, on the occasion, Robert Carlson noted, "Our stores never looked better. We have the opportunity to make every shopper a Crowley's shopper." Significantly, Crowley's employment jumped from about 1,700 to above 2,000 in 1985 and grew even more after the new 1986 stores opened. *Metropolitan Detroit* magazine hailed the progress made by Carlson and his team at Crowley's, saying:

> *A few years ago, it was considered by some industry analysts to be one more department store elephant lumbering to the graveyard. Today, a slimmed-down Crowley's is sprinting like a gazelle and heading toward the greatest*

earnings in the company's history. President Robert Carlson explains: "You can't be all things to all people, so we decided to define what we do well and do it while we tried to become more efficient in people, time, and space."

With all of the positive activity, Crowley's stock price rose dramatically, and in late 1986, Robert Carlson and Crowley treasurer Andrew Soffel announced they were putting together a leveraged buyout of the ascendant company but were ultimately unable to find financing to pull the deal off and buy a controlling interest in Crowley's. The store remained 51 percent owned by Joseph Crowley's grandchildren Joann (Standart) Cousino, Joseph and Richard Keys and Patricia (Standart) Morrison.

Many shoppers and employees well remember Crowley's in this era as an alternative to Hudson's or just a pleasant place to shop. Given the generosity of the firm, it remained a good place to work and still delivered a level of customer service fitting the stores historic "friendly" image. Teresa Serra Czarnecki recalls, "I worked at Crowley's in Livonia Mall, Farmington, Tel-Twelve and also at the opening day of the Westland store. I'm sure I still have my name badge, cards and envelopes to send out to clients, a pen and a Halloween Bag that I hang on to because they all hold such good memories."

When profits for 1986 dropped to $1.8 million from the record-setting levels of 1985, it was felt that it was a temporary setback mostly resulting from opening three new stores in rapid succession. As 1987 progressed, though, it was clear that Crowley's was losing significant amounts of money and sales were sliding. The management's response was to close the Grand River store and slash payroll through layoffs. A visible sign of the financial trouble at the venerable store was the cancellation of its sponsorship of the Grand Marshal's float in Detroit's annual Thanksgiving Day parade.

In addition, Crowley family heiress Patricia Standart Morrison broke from her sister and cousins by resigning from Crowley's board and eventually selling her 12.9 percent share in the store's ownership. Morrison never worked at Crowley's and lived in Tennessee, where she invested in the Cedar Run Club and Retreat, an event venue in Seymour, Tennessee. Leigh Morrison recalls, "There was some disagreement between my mother and her sister and cousins about the selling of the store stock. My mom was in the midst of purchasing a large farm, which she used for a restaurant/corporate retreat center." As a result, the remaining heirs saw their ownership drop to 38 percent.

Losses for 1987 amounted to $1.9 million, and the *Detroit News* called Crowley's "beleaguered" and reported that it was looking for a buyer. To counter the rumors, Richard Keys told the *Detroit News*, "We're sticking with

Crowley's. We feel the thing to do is to get the company turned around. We feel we've got the management team in place to do it." His brother, Joseph, added, "We're not looking for any buyers. We'd listen to an offer, but we are not actively soliciting any."

It became clear that Carlson's program attempted to achieve too much change too soon and that Crowley's trade-up came along just as the Detroit market welcomed new Mervyn's, Target and Main Street stores, later bought by popular-price retailer Kohl's. The results of all the new competition were disastrous for Crowley's. Steve Kennedy, as vice-president of operations, watched the implementation of the failed strategy, saying, "Carlson really didn't get into the nitty gritty. At the same time the store was taken upscale, not enough attention was paid to merchandising. The biggest complaint was the merchandise itself and how badly it was distributed. If you were looking for a pair of pants at Macomb Mall, for instance, we'd have twenty-eight-inch waist and fifty-inch waist models, but customers couldn't find anything in between, which were incidentally the most popular sizes. That was a chronic problem and there was no solution in sight."

In 1988, Carlson was succeeded by former treasurer Andrew Soffel as president. Soffel was known as a hardline financial manager, and he attempted get the losses under control while bringing Crowley's merchandise policy back to its earlier strong selling point—moderately priced clothing. However, sales declined as the country slid into a deep recession, and by 1991, Crowley's had hired Kidder, Peabody & Co. to find a partner that could buy the chain and infuse funds to bring it back to profitability. Significantly, Soffel slashed the store's dividend in half, something Crowley's had not done before. With losses totaling $2.5 million in 1990, Soffel further cut staff and fired management that had come to Crowley's under Robert Carlson's leadership. Joyce Harding, former vice-president of merchandising who lost her job when Soffel cut management, responded by telling the *Detroit Free Press*, "To me, Crowley's doesn't stand for anything. It never has, and it never will."

Under Soffel's leadership, the store did try to improve assortments and tried new concepts in order to pull itself out of the doldrums. A handsome, freestanding men's store was opened in the Tel-Twelve mall, freeing up space in the existing store for an expanded selection of home furnishings merchandise. The success of the men's store led to the eventual opening of another one in Farmington Hills. But the overall picture remained bleak. When the previous effort to find a buyer for the chain resulted in failure, investment banking firm First of Michigan Corporation was engaged to try again, but this time, Soffel told stockholders at the store's annual meeting that a buyout or merger were about the only ways out for the struggling company.

Crowley's hired former Hess's (of Allentown, Pennsylvania) senior vice-president Denny Callahan as CEO in 1992. Callahan came on board just as bankruptcy loomed. Crowley's needed a loan of $8 million to survive, but even longstanding Detroit bank Comerica considered any loan to Crowley's too great of a risk. Callahan, known as a turnaround specialist, went to work cutting management, consolidating operations and closing the Westland store, which had never been profitable. Regarding Crowley's desperate need for operating funds, Callahan turned to Schottenstein Stores of Columbus, Ohio, which provided the firm with the $8 million it needed to remain in operation.

Schottenstein, which operated Value City department stores in various states, had a reputation for acquiring distressed retailers, liquidating them and converting locations to its Value City format. The well-respected Lamson's of Toledo and the Halle Brothers Company of Cleveland were among the stores acquired and closed by Schottenstein, and it will be recalled that Detroit's Ernst Kern Company was purchased by Schottenstein Stores just before it went out of business in 1959.

Steve Kennedy left Crowley's in 1989 after twenty-five years with the company. "I was driving to Port Huron to look at a potential store location, when I got sick on the expressway in the middle of nowhere. I had no phone; there were no cops around, so I inched the car home and collapsed. The next thing you know, I was in Henry Ford Hospital and learned I had suffered a small stroke." When his doctor told him that he could go back to work but would be dead within a year, Kennedy thought about his family. "I didn't want to put my wife through that. In addition, I had a shitty childhood, and now I had six sons at home and didn't want to miss good times with my grandchildren." He told Joseph Keys about his decision to leave when the Crowley family heir came into his office. "He told me he had just come in to offer me the presidency. For the longest time, I dreamed of getting to the top—but man plans, God laughs, I guess!"

Over his life, Kennedy's family orientation clearly gave him the love and support he missed in the childhood he spoke about. It's important to add an anecdote Kennedy revealed about his family in order to understand the nature of this man and his role at Crowley's:

> *Because of my time as a foster child, my wife and I decided to take children in need, too. We were contacted by Catholic Social Services about a special*

needs boy who had no home, so, of course, we took him. A funny thing happened, though. They kept calling us, telling us that they were sure they could find a permanent place for this boy, if we could only keep him for another two months. Over time, it kept happening, and eventually, the whole family bonded with him. One day at dinner, I just said, "Anybody who wants Jay to be their brother, raise your hands!" My five sons raised their hands, so we just adopted him and it was one of the best things we ever did.

After Kennedy left Crowley's in 1989, he kept an eye on things as an outsider. "I wasn't involved anymore, but I could see where it was going. Callahan was capable, but he was feared, and he got tied up with Schottenstein, who are a tough bunch of people. It was like stepping into a trap." After Crowley's repaid the Schottenstein loan, it entered a deal with the Ohio company to finance the acquisition of Steinbach stores of New Jersey. In return for the loan, Schottenstein got 45 percent ownership of Crowley's. Interestingly, Schottenstein was the owner of the Steinbach chain when the stores were acquired by Crowley's.

Closed by the time Crowley's acquired the chain, Steinbach's Asbury Park flagship had a great history in its community, just as Crowley's did in Detroit. In Steinbach's case, though, the building was saved and renovated into residences. *Courtesy of Don Stine.*

The Steinbach Company was founded in Asbury Park, New Jersey, in 1870 by namesake John Steinbach. In the 1890s, he built a large, wedge-shaped, four-story department store (later augmented with a fifth floor) that became a shopping landmark in the resort, if not all of Monmouth County, in which it was located. Eventually, the store opened branches all along the New Jersey shore and was, at one time, part of the small chain

Here are two examples of the New Jersey Steinbach stores that Crowley's acquired. *Top*: Steinbach in the 1973 Manalapan Mall. *Bottom*: An interior view of the Shore Mall location in Egg Harbor. *Courtesy of Michael Lisicky.*

of upscale department stores owned by the S.S. Kresge Company, which included the Kresge-Newark store in New Jersey's largest city; Palais Royal in Washington, D.C.; and the Fair of Chicago.

Similar to Crowley's, the Steinbach Company grew to become a respected regional department store, but hard times in Asbury Park (including 1970 race riots like those experienced three years earlier in Detroit) forced the flagship store to close in July 1979. From that time on, Steinbach transformed itself into a fashion specialty store. Owned by Supermarkets General Corporation since 1960, Steinbach acquired Connecticut retail nameplates Howland's and Genung's; Goerke's of Elizabeth, New Jersey; and New York off-price retailer Ohrbach's. When Crowley's purchased the chain, Schottenstein (which bought Steinbach in 1994) kept four locations as Value City discount stores, and the Detroit-based store got the other sixteen stores throughout the Northeast.

It all looked rosy at the time. Crowley's doubled its sales figures as a result of the acquisition and cut operating costs by consolidating key operations such as buying, distribution and advertising in Detroit. Profits rose over $1 million as a result of the deal. Steve Kennedy, now looking at it from outside, had a different opinion, however.

You can look like a hero by buying a chain of stores, and combining the operations. Of course it increased profits in the first year. It was like found money. Sooner or later, the problems of distributing merchandise to the East Coast from Detroit, let alone shipping it across those distances, becomes a difficult proposition. The prevailing attitude was the "we'll handle it later." In the second year, reality sets in. And that's exactly what happened.

The quick accumulation of profits surprised even veteran Detroit area–based retail analyst Fred Marx, who exclaimed, "Crowley's defies gravity!" In 1997, the Birmingham store landlord decided to redevelop the property, forcing the closure of Crowley's branch in the upscale suburb. Callahan announced a plan for Crowley's to acquire Detroit's foundering Winkelman's women's fashion stores and tried opening prototype specialty stores selling women's clothing ("Sarah's by Crowley's) and freestanding home stores. It also expanded the fairly successful Shops of New Center One location by moving into adjacent lease spaces.

While 1997 was a year of optimism for Crowley's, in 1998, it was revealed that the store lost an astronomical $6.54 million in the first six months of the year. At the end of the year, Schottenstein Stores

Crowley's added an upscale men's store to its Tel-Twelve location, clearly reflecting Robert Carlson's ideas for Crowley's. *Courtesy of László Regös.*

announced that it had taken control of Crowley's in a complicated stock swap that resulted in the dismissal of Denny Callahan and the substitution of Lance Wimmer of Dallas, Texas, as Crowley's new CEO. Wimmer was described as a "turnaround expert" by Schottenstein. But the *Detroit Free Press*, at the time of the takeover, reported that Amber Stores, an arts-and-crafts retailer, had filed for bankruptcy in 1995 after Wimmer became CEO and he was recently dismissed from a similar position at Image Dynamics of Grand Prairie, Texas, a photo booth manufacturer, after a year of disappointing results.

Judy Bonin, a native of Ubly, Michigan, who was an avid Crowley's shopper before retiring to Florida, voiced her opinion about the Crowley's debacle. "Crowley's always did well until they got involved with that hillbilly. That was the end of it," she says. And she wasn't far from the truth. On January 21, 1999, Crowley's laid off the majority of its employees, mostly without severance pay, and benefits were scheduled to be canceled within a few days of the sacking. Lance Wimmer stayed on throughout the liquidation process and was paid $2,000 per day according to the *Detroit News* for his services, though amounts such as that were not actually considered unusual. In February, the store filed for bankruptcy protection.

Just before Crowley's folded, it did a top-to-bottom rehab of the Macomb Mall store. Sadly, it was all for nothing, and the discount racks of Value City were moved in shortly thereafter. The Crowley's logo in the floor remained, but anything else reminiscent of the historic department store was gone for good. *Courtesy of László Regös.*

Liquidation followed, and remaining stores were sold off. Hudson's took Crowley's only major mall location at Lakeside Mall in Sterling Heights to remodel and reopen the store as a men's and home furnishings branch, leaving its original 214,000-square-foot store in the mall to concentrate on women's and children's clothing. The Bon Ton stores of York, Pennsylvania, bid on some Steinbach locations, and Value City itself eyed the Westborn, Macomb, Livonia and Universal Mall stores for its own use. However, many of Crowley's stores went unwanted. Ironically, the Macomb Mall store had just undergone a drastic renovation just as the chain folded. Well-known photographer László Regös had just completed an extensive photo shoot of the store, which included a children's play area and a coffee bar, when "just like that they filed for bankruptcy and I never got paid for my work."

The bankruptcy was settled by April 1999, and it was announced that Value City department stores would open later in the year at three locations that once belonged to Crowley's. To soften the blow to Detroit residents with a soft spot for Crowley's, the stores would be known as Crowley's Value City. It was no use, though. After a flurry of excitement on the occasion of the reopening in August, the Value City concept never really caught on, and the stores' cluttered atmosphere and flea-market look turned off anyone who remembered Crowley's.

Shopper Judy Bonin relates an experience at the Macomb Mall Value City store:

So Ken [her husband] *and I went in there and found a couple of things to buy. We had to wait in two parallel lines at the mall exit, since they only had two checkout counters. The clerks were slow, and the lines were long. After waiting in line for quite a while, there were just two customers in front of us, and when the girl at the register finished up with one of them, she said "I'm closing. You people will just have to go get in the other line." The guy in front of us told her, "The f*** you are!" and she snapped back at him, "The f*** I'm not!!" We just put our stuff down and got the hell out of there!*

Detroit's Friendly Store was a thing of the past.

Opposite, bottom: Even the exterior of the Macomb Mall store received a face-lifted canopy in the 1999 upgrade. The building was eventually replaced by a big-box retailer after Value City pulled out of the shopping center. *Courtesy of László Regös.*

CROWLEY'S DOWNTOWN STORE DIRECTORY

MAIN BUILDING

Basement

Crowley's Budget Store • Basement Cafeteria • Soda Fountain • Snack Bar • Shoe Repair

Street Floor

Fine Jewelry (Department 133) • Better Jewelry (Department 19) • Costume Jewelry (Department 19) • Handbags (Department 21) • Small Leather Goods (Department 21) • Gloves (Department 7) • Scarves (Department 26) • Hat Bar (Department 184) • Hosiery (Department 14) • Wonderful World of Beauty (Department 17) • Blouses (Department 22) • Sweaters (Department 22) • Career Sportswear (Department 22) • Street Floor Lingerie • Notions (Department 15) • Candy • Stationery Office Equipment (Department 89) • Red Cross Shoes • Drugs (Department 17) • Gourmet Shop (Department 3)

Mezzanine

Books (Department 30) • Luggage (Department 4) • Cameras (Department 41) • Record Shop • Engraved Stationery • Jewelry Repair • Religious Articles • Drugs • Pharmacy • Optical • Beauty Salon • Chiropody • Travel Service • Mezzanine Tea Room

Appendix A

Second Floor

Children's Wear (Department 56) • Infants and Toddlers (Department 39) • Girl's Wear (Department 68) • Young Girls' Wear (Department 58) • Children's Shoes (Department 75) • Children's Furniture (Department 63) • Shoe Salon (Department 40) • Gift Wrapping Service

Third Floor

Misses' Dresses (Department 60) • Misses' Sportswear (Department 42) • Coats and Suits (Department 36, 37) • Renbrooke Fur Salon (Department 137) • Talk of the Town • Cosmopolitan Shop (Department 79) • The Expressionist Shop • Bridal Shop • Young Idea Shop (Department 52) • Career Dresses (Department 53) • Custom Shop (Department 80) • Women's Sportswear (Department 60) • Millinery (Department 183) • Junior Sportswear (Department 69) • Junior Dresses (Department 81) • Junior Coats (Department 72) • Young Juniors (Department 64) • Maternity Shop

Fourth Floor

Robes (Department 66) • Nightwear (Department 7) • Daytime Lingerie (Department 38) • Loungewear (Department 66) • Foundations (Department 67) • Linens (Department 6) • Domestics (Department 9, 10) • Bath Boutique Shop (Department 6) • Sewing Center (Department 140) • Fabrics (Department 8) • Art Needlework (Department 6) • Tree Lane (Department 61)

Fifth Floor

Housewares (Department 1) • Creative Cookery Gourmet Shop (Department 1) • Hardware (Department 47) • Appliances (Department 57) • China (Department 5) • Table Linens (Department 12) • Glassware • Silver • Gift Shop • Music Center (Department 20) • Records (Department 161) • Televisions (Department 20) • Pet Supplies • Gems of the World • Garden Shop

Sixth Floor

Draperies (Department 46) • Curtains (Department 46) • Lamps (Department 59) • Pictures • Mirrors (Department 59) • Floor Coverings (Department 45) • Rugs (Department 45) • Toys (Department 2) • Sporting Goods (Department 2) • Casual Furniture • Trim-a-Home Shop (Department 61)

Seventh Floor

Furniture (Department 48) • Sleep Center (Department 90) • Interior Decorating Service • Credit Office

Eighth Floor

Display Department

East Building

Street Floor

Men's Furnishings (Department 27) • Men's Sportswear (Department 98)

Second Floor

Men's Clothing (Department 71) • Young Men's Shop (Department 94) • Men's Shoes • Men's Hats • Boys' Wear (Department 33)

Third Floor

Stock and service area

Fourth Floor

Children's Play Room

Fifth Floor

Cash Office

Sixth Floor

Christmas Toyland

Seventh Floor

Auditorium

APPENDIX A

Eighth Floor

Advertising • Executive Offices • Employment Office • Public Relations • Purchasing

Ninth Floor

Personal Shopping Service—Kay Graham

Tenth Floor

Stock and service area

Eleventh Floor

Hospital

CROWLEY'S STORE LOCATIONS

DOWNTOWN

100–26 Gratiot Avenue
Detroit, Michigan
July 1908
793,934 square feet

WESTBORN

23303 Michgan Avenue
Dearborn, Michigan
February 26, 1959
106,000 square feet

GRAND RIVER

15270 Grand River Avenue
Detroit, Michigan
March 10, 1960
45,000 square feet

MACOMB MALL

32385 Gratiot Avenue
Roseville, Michigan
October 29, 1964
127,000 square feet

LIVONIA MALL

29560 Seven Mile Road
Livonia, Michigan
October 29, 1964
127,000 square feet

NEW CENTER

6433 Woodward Avenue
Detroit, Michigan
August 3, 1972
60,000 square feet

BIRMINGHAM

200 North Woodward
Birmingham, Michigan
August 14, 1972
69,000 square feet

FARMINGTON

Kendallwood Shopping Center
33250 West Twelve Mile Road
Farmington Hills, Michigan
August 3, 1972
85,000 square feet

LAKESIDE MALL

14150 Lakeside Circle
Sterling Heights, Michigan
September 11, 1975
115,000 square feet

ARBORLAND

Washtenaw Road
Ann Arbor, Michigan
1980
46,000 square feet

UNIVERSAL MALL

28300 Dequindre Road
Warren, Michigan
1980
102,000 square feet

TEL-TWELVE MALL

29694 Telegraph Road
Southfield, Michigan
1985
57,000 square feet

COURTLAND CENTER

4424 Court Street
Burton, Michigan
August 11, 1986
61,000 square feet

New Center One

3031 West Grand Boulevard
Detroit, Michigan
August 18, 1986
49,000 square feet

Wildwood Center

Westland Michigan
October 30, 1986
58,000 square feet

CROWLEY FAMILY TREE

CROWLEY, Cornelius (March 15, 1822–February 6, 1895) m. Catherine Bresnahan (1833–October 13, 1901)
91 Porter Street, Detroit
    CROWLEY, Joseph Jeremiah (April 26, 1862–November 1, 1925) m. Jennie E. Flynn (April 1, 1870–August 19, 1956)
    243 Lakeland Avenue, Grosse Pointe
        CROWLEY, Helen m. John G. Keys
            Keys, Joseph C.
            Keys, Richard S.
        CROWLEY, Marjorie (1907–1969) m. David G. Standart (1909–1983)
            Standart, Joanne (1939–) m. Raymond Cousino (1941–)
            Standart, Patricia Ann (1940–2009) m. Richard Bruce Morrison (1939–)
        CROWLEY, Katherine (1894–1981) m. De Hull N. Travis (1882–1960)
        CROWLEY, Daniel J. (June 14, 1892–February 10, 1957)
        CROWLEY, Joseph J. (June 10, 1900–March 27, 1913)

    CROWLEY, Daniel T. (March 13, 1864–April 6, 1936) m. Mary Dwyer
    203 Lakeland Avenue, Grosse Pointe
        CROWLEY, Marion m. James M. Campbell

APPENDIX C

CROWLEY, William C. (February 13, 1866—February 19, 1927)
m. Elizabeth Sullivan Freeman (1879–1931)
44 Beverly Road, Grosse Pointe
>CROWLEY, Elizabeth Evans m. Haywood Dana Newbold
>CROWLEY, Catherine Hungerford m. William Cushman

BIBLIOGRAPHY

Austin, Dan. *Forgotten Landmarks of Detroit*. Charleston, SC: The History Press, 2012.

Burton, Clarence Monroe, and William Stocking. *The City of Detroit, Michigan, 1701–1922*. Detroit, MI: S.J. Clarke Publishing Company, 1922.

Ferry, John William. *A History of the Department Store*. New York: Macmillan Company, 1960.

Hauser, Michael, and Marianne Weldon. *Twentieth-Century Retailing in Downtown Detroit*. Charleston, SC: Arcadia Publishing, 2008.

Hawkins, Ferry W. *The Buildings of Detroit: A History*. Detroit, MI: Wayne State University Press, 1968.

Hendrickson, Robert. *The Grand Emporiums*. New York: Stein and Day, 1979.

Holleman, Thomas. *Smith, Hinchman & Grylls: 125 Years of Architecture & Engineering, 1853–1978*. Detroit, MI: Wayne State University Press, 1968.

Longstreth, Richard. *The American Department Store Transformed, 1920–1960*. New Haven, CT: Yale University Press, 2010.

BIBLIOGRAPHY

Marquis, Albert. *The Book of Detroiters*. Chicago: A.N. Marquis & Co., 1914.

Pirone, Fran. *Stores of the Year 1979–1980*. New York: Retail Reporting Bureau, 1979.

Pitrone, Jean. *Hudson's: Hub of America's Heartland*. West Bloomfield, MI: Altwerger and Mandel Publishing Co., 1991.

Redstone, Louis G. *New Dimensions in Shopping Centers and Stores*. New York: McGraw Hill, Inc., 1973.

Whitaker, Jan. *The World of Department Stores*. New York: Vendome Press, 2011.

INDEX

ABOUT THE AUTHOR

*B*ruce Allen Kopytek came to be an author almost accidentally while searching for new opportunities when his career as an architect imploded as a result of the Great Recession, figuring that one day his status as an admitted and gleefully unrepentant "book-a-holic" would lead him to writing. A completely unexpected offer to write his first book, the award-winning *Jacobson's: I Miss It So!*, focused his attention on another of his favorite subjects: the life and times of North America's great, beloved and long-gone department stores.

Now vice-president of commercial architecture at Fieldstone Architecture

Photo by Drew Mason.

& Engineering of Auburn Hills, Michigan, Kopytek credits his parents and his close-knit family with his passions for travel, history and art. His parents placed education and their faith on a high pedestal and fostered both of these elements in their family through frequent travel and interest in culture in all its aspects.

About the Author

For the Kopytek family, life was experienced together—and on quite a high plane at that.

Taking cues from his past, Kopytek has traveled throughout North America and Europe and happily rediscovered his extended family across the Atlantic in Poland as result. In architecture, he considers himself a jack-of-all-trades who must be ready to fulfill any task that might present itself, whether artistic or practical. Along with a resurgent career, he is also proud of his reinvigorated and long-held religious faith.

With his wife, Carole, he enjoys traveling, ballroom dancing, lecturing on topics related to his books, cooking and doing volunteer work through his local Roman Catholic parish, St. Lawrence, in Utica, Michigan. He cherishes his family and remains not only close with his sister, Mary, and brother, Patrick, and their children but also takes delight in his relationship with Jesse and Jennifer, the adult children he inherited when he married again after living as a widower for ten years.

All of these things are the mise-en-scène for Kopytek's own pursuits in architecture and writing, and he considers them vital ingredients in life's mission. He lives happily with his wife, Carole, in a town house far north of his native Hamtramck, Michigan, along with Bella, their pastel calico cat, who loves to talk and rewards Kopytek and his wife for their good behavior by presenting them with one of her feathered cat toys, dragged noisily up or down the stairs, confirming that she is indeed the de facto ruler of their home.